GO GLUTEN AND DAIRY FREE AND FEEL GREAT!

GISELLE WRIGLEY
BSc (Hons) Pharmacy

Go Gluten and Dairy Free and Feel Great! –

Published by Giselle Wrigley

Cover and text design by ebook-designs.co.uk

Text copyright © Giselle Wrigley 2015

Giselle Wrigley has asserted her right under the Copyright, Designs and Patents Act 1988 to be identified as the author of this work.

A CIP record for this book is available from the British Library.

CONTENTS

INTRODUCTION

Welcome to your guide to going gluten and dairy free. You may have longstanding allergies or coeliac disease or you may just be at the point of suspecting that your medical symptoms are food related; either way this book is for you.

I suffer myself with both allergies (nuts – diagnosed as a child) and intolerances (wheat and dairy –diagnosed in my thirties). One of my daughters also suffers with allergies to dairy but neither my husband nor my other child do.

As a busy mother and pharmacist with two businesses, I found the challenge of cooking healthy, free-from food for my family quite overwhelming. Without the right advice, going dairy and gluten- free can be all-consuming and easily turn feeding your family into a full-time job.

This book is the one I would like to have read myself when I was first coming to grips with going gluten and dairy free. It is not only full of practical advice but also a number of QUICK, EASY and HEALTHY recipes.

In **Part One** of this book I explain the difference between allergies and intolerances, what causes them, how to get diagnosed, and most importantly how to treat them.

In **Part Two** I talk you through the most recent advice on healthy eating, which vitamin supplements are beneficial for people with gluten and dairy sensitivities, and why.

In **Part Three**, I give you simple recipes that your whole family will want to eat which are free from dairy and gluten (most are also free from nuts, soya, and eggs too).

Feel free to dip in and out of the sections that interest you – each part can be read in isolation.

My story

This book has come about through years of interest in nutrition and personal experience of dietary issues. Allergies and intolerances affect people differently, but there is no doubt that until you have them under control, they have a significant impact on health and well-being.

My journey into allergies started at age five when I asked my parents for a treat at the supermarket. The brand of chocolate I chose contained nuts, and we spent a fraught evening in A&E after my face ballooned to the size of a watermelon within seconds of ingesting the offending item.

People who have allergies often present what is known as an 'atopic' range of conditions. If you have atopy, you have either eczema, asthma or hay fever (or some combination thereof), and are typically predisposed to allergies. Atopy runs in families; my dad has hay fever and I suffered as a child with eczema, asthma and allergies to nuts, sesame seeds, eggs, dust and animals. As an adult, my allergies and asthma were manageable and I 'grew out' of my eczema and egg allergy. So far so good; however, in my thirties I then began my journey into the world of food intolerance – my problems here are with gluten and dairy.

I am not alone with this as it is an increasingly common problem for many. Figures released by Allergy UK say that up to 45% of the population claim they suffer with food intolerance at some time, and the main offenders are thought to be gluten and dairy.[1,2] Until recently, food intolerance was often dismissed by the medical community: diagnosis is difficult and medics are understandably cautious about recommending cutting whole food groups out of the diet without good reason.

Novak Jokcovic, the world's current number one tennis player, with 6 grand slams and 14 Masters titles to his name, suffers with a gluten intolerance that went undiagnosed for years. He was plagued with chest pain, stomach spasms and fatigue that he just couldn't get to the bottom of and which affected his game significantly. It wasn't until a Serbian doctor diagnosed him as gluten intolerant in 2010 and completely overhauled his diet that he was finally relieved of his symptoms; he describes the change in how he feels now he is gluten free as 'like magic.'[3]

Symptoms of intolerance can be wide-ranging and can be anything from gastrointestinal symptoms to joint pain, skin problems, headaches and fatigue. It is important to note here how crucial it is to get medical help if you do suspect food intolerance and haven't been diagnosed; you cannot presume medical symptoms are food related – other underlying medical issues must always be checked out first.

Personally, my issues with intolerance started after two particularly difficult pregnancies where I had suffered with hyperemesis (leading me to vomit 12-14 times a day for 9 long months), and symptoms were mainly gastrointestinal plus exhaustion. I am quite a get-up-and-go person, so at first I just put it down to parenthood and having small children (sleep deprivation is a form of torture after all – anyone not sleeping for four years wouldn't expect to be on best form!). My GP did send me for an appointment with a consultant gastroenterologist, but both an ultrasound test and gastroscopy camera revealed nothing.

In the interim, a friend of mine had been to see a naturopathic practitioner and recommended this particular practitioner highly. I went to see her, explained my symptoms, had a Vega test done (which I was very sceptical about) but duly cut out gluten, dairy and caffeine from my diet as this test had recommended. Well, if Novak describes his experience as magic; I remember describing mine as a 'miracle' (and I don't use that word lightly). Having lived for such a long time feeling as I had done, the fact that my symptoms cleared up after four weeks of simply abstaining from certain foods was miraculous to me. The gastric consultant I saw subsequently (to marvel about my discovery with!) did concede that caffeine is a gastric irritant but was rather dismissive of my other claims about gluten as my blood tests had come back negative for coeliac disease. Nonetheless, I was cock-a-hoop as I had found a new lease of life and finally felt like myself again.

Around this time, I also discovered that my daughter is allergic to milk (she started having problems when she was weaned from breastfeeding onto formula milk at around six months old). Despite all my previous experience with allergies, it still took us until she was nine months old to get a diagnosis; the information out there was overwhelming and conflicting at best.

You would think I may have had a head start with all of this in that I am medically trained as a pharmacist and have always had a specialist interest in nutrition. Whilst at university, I not only studied pure pharmaceutical science but also took all the elective courses in natural medicine and must have read every book and guideline ever issued on healthy eating. (When working as a pharmacist for Boots I was even the 'Vitamins Champion'!) So you would think I would be able to make sense quite quickly of the plethora of information, and know what to do not only to get diagnosed but also how to deal with dairy and gluten-free eating on a day to day basis. However, the more you look into allergies and intolerances, the more you realise just how much we have still to learn about these conditions. After five years of research, reading, and asking a variety of health professionals' advice (including GPs, immunology consultants, dieticians, and naturopathic medical practitioners), this book is my summary of what is currently known and understood by the medical community about both allergies and intolerances, and most importantly, WHAT TO DO ABOUT IT!

I sincerely hope that reading it helps you as much as writing it has helped me.

PART ONE: THE SCIENCE BEHIND ALLERGIES AND INTOLERANCES EXPLAINED

ALLERGIES

Definition – what is an allergy?

Allergies are typically defined as an immediate immune response to what the body perceives to be a 'foreign substance'. Immune system antibodies called 'Immunoglobulin E' (or IgE) are released in response to the allergen and provoke a histamine reaction in the body resulting in symptoms such as wheezing, itching, swelling and rashes.[1]

Prevalence – how many people suffer with allergies?

Allergies are becoming much more prevalent and rates of food allergies have risen sharply in the last 20 years.[2] According to the NHS website, 5-8% of young children and 3-4% of adults have a food allergy in the UK.[3]

Types of foods that cause allergies

Any food can cause an allergy although the most common offenders are:

- Cow's milk or goat and sheep milk (do not use these as substitutes for cow's milk)

- Soy (10% of people allergic to milk are also allergic to soy so it is important not to just swap to a soy-based diet)

- Gluten (gluten is a protein found in grains like wheat, rye, barley and sometimes oats. So you can be allergic to wheat on its own or you can be allergic to gluten, which means you have to avoid wheat, barley, rye and be careful what brand of oats you buy)

- Egg

- Peanuts

- Tree nuts (e.g. walnuts or cashew nuts)

- Seeds (such as sesame seeds)

- Fish and shellfish

- Celery

- Mustard

- Sulphur dioxide and sulphites (these are preservatives often found in things like dried fruit or wine)[4]

Why do we get allergies? The Hygiene Hypothesis

Is it still largely unknown why people develop allergies to food, although a proportion of the population are genetically predisposed to allergies; these people are known as 'atopic' and may also have other conditions such as asthma, hay fever or eczema.[5]

Members of the medical community do have one theory to explain why there has been such a surge in the prevalence of allergies over the last 20-30 years and they call it the 'hygiene hypothesis'. This theory suggests a link between low levels of exposure to micro-organisms and the development of autoimmune conditions such as allergies. The blame falls on overuse of antibiotics, insufficient exposure to the outdoors (we don't let our children play in the dirt like they used to) and overuse of chemical cleaning products: we are just too hygienic.[6]

The idea is that in order for our immune system to develop properly, we need a certain amount of low level 'challenge' from bacteria in our environment. Without this low level challenge to set the bar, the immune system 'over-reacts' when it comes into contact with what should be harmless foodstuffs, but which the allergic person's body now sees as a threat.

Just to clarify, the idea is *not* that hygiene in general is bad: no one doubts that a certain level of hygiene is essential, and certainly sanitation and the advent of vaccines means that there are no longer epidemics in the western world from diseases such as cholera and typhoid. However, killing all our 'good bacteria' along with the 'bad bacteria' seems to have had repercussions for our immune system.[7]

The hygiene hypothesis is just a theory at the moment, but it is the best one we have. When you talk to naturopathic doctors about allergies, they also consider concepts such as the 'leaky gut', which suggests that large particles of food enter the bloodstream via the gut. This theory states that due to a damaged or inflamed intestinal lining some people don't digest their food properly, leading to large molecules entering the bloodstream which the immune system sees as a threat, and mounts an 'over-reactive' response to.[8] Mainstream medics don't buy into this as they say the lining of the gut is not permeable in that way,[9] but there is no doubt among anyone that for whatever reason, allergies, intolerances (and inflammatory diseases) are on the increase in the western world.[10]

Diagnosis

Allergies are relatively easy to diagnose compared with intolerances; this can be done by a skin prick test, a blood test or a food challenge test, and your first port of call to access these tests is your **GP**. The three tests are described below:

1. A **skin prick test** is often the first to be done and involves pricking your skin with a tiny amount of the allergen to see if there is a reaction. If there is, the skin around the prick will become itchy and a red wheal (swelling) will appear. The severity of the reaction can be measured using a test or 'control' prick and measuring the size of the wheal that appears in comparison to the control. These tests can be useful for giving a general indication of allergy, but doctors treat them with caution as false positives occur in nearly half of cases (in other words, you react to the test but aren't actually allergic to that particular substance). Negative tests are considered 95% accurate; if you don't react at all it is a good sign that you aren't allergic.[11]

2. The **blood test for allergens** is formally known as a RAST test and measures the level of Immunoglobulin E (IgE) antibodies that appear in your bloodstream when you have been exposed to the allergen. Again, IgE testing is fairly conclusive for a negative result (about 90% accuracy), but just above 50% reliability for positive results.[12]

3. A **food challenge** is the most accurate way to diagnose a food allergy – during the test you are given the food which you

think you are allergic to in increasing amounts to see how you react. Doctors monitor you for signs of allergy including pupil dilation, rashes, swelling, increased heart rate etc.

For those people with immediate response allergies, it is fairly obvious when a foodstuff has caused a reaction; most allergy sufferers identify with the feeling straight away. For those with delayed allergic reactions the picture is more complicated, as delayed allergic reactions still have IgE mediated responses (so the immune system is involved) but because the symptoms appear later it can be difficult to distinguish which food is causing the allergy. It is important that you speak to your doctor regarding the above methods of diagnoses.

Treatment

For patients with severe allergies, the best treatment is to avoid the allergen for life.

Some patients experience mild symptoms (rashes and a tingling sensation in the mouth) which can be controlled with anti-histamine medication or inhalers for those with asthmatic symptoms. Other patients have severe, life-threatening reactions, and these patients are advised to carry an adrenaline injection (called an EpiPen) with them wherever they go. Anaphylaxis can affect a number of the body's systems including the skin (causing swelling and rashes), the cardiovascular system (leading to increased heart rate), the gastrointestinal system (causing nausea, vomiting and diarrhoea), the respiratory system (causing problems breathing) and the central nervous system (including confusion, headache and loss of consciousness).[13]Patients presenting with these symptoms are advised to seek emergency medical attention.

Unfortunately, reactions can vary between exposures and are not always dose related. Just because you had a mild reaction previously, doesn't mean that you won't have a more serious reaction the next time.[14]This means people with allergies must be constantly vigilant.

Outgrowing allergies

Sometimes children who are diagnosed with allergies as babies will outgrow them later on. Most children who have food allergies to milk, eggs, soya or wheat in early life will outgrow the allergy by the time they are five years old. The reason for this is unknown, but it is thought to be associated with the maturation of the digestive system or a change in the child's immune response to the food.[15]

Allergies to nuts, seeds or shellfish tend to be lifelong allergies and it is uncommon to grow out of these.[16]

A statistic which illustrates this well is that 80% of children with peanut allergies will remain allergic to them for life, whereas 80% of children with milk allergy will outgrow it by the time they go to school.[17]

Building tolerance

The most recent thinking for the treatment of children with allergies to milk, eggs, soya or wheat (allergens which are more common to grow out of) is to encourage the child to ingest very small amounts of the allergenic substance on a daily basis with the theory that it will build the body's tolerance to the item and that in time, the body will become used to it.[18,19,20,21]

However, there is a balancing act when it comes to allergen exposure as, once your body has been exposed to the allergen, it is difficult to predict how well or how badly you will react with subsequent exposure. Sometimes, an exposure can send your body into 'overdrive' or 'high alert', and even a minor subsequent exposure can produce severe reactions. The medical community has no way of understanding or predicting what your particular sensitivity is; your body may react by 'tolerating' the allergen and not reacting as badly next time, or it may have the opposite effect and, if you become 'sensitised', you could have a very extreme reaction the next time. For this reason, caution must be used when deciding to undergo tolerance therapy, and certainly tolerance programs for allergens such as milk or wheat must be done under medical supervision.

An interesting aside is the much-publicised recent study on patients with a life-threatening peanut allergy. This showed that giving patients very, very small doses of peanuts over a prolonged period of time (starting with a grain of peanut flour and working up to three peanuts a day) enables patients to tolerate them.[22] The idea of building tolerance for this group of patients is that if they come into contact with the allergen by accident, their body won't over-react and send the patient into anaphylactic shock; this could be revolutionary for the lives of those patients who have extreme reactions to allergens. The study showed, however, that it was important to expose the body to the allergen *every* day in order for the benefit to persist.

It is important to reiterate here that with respect to food allergies, it is only allergies to milk, wheat, soya, and egg that it is considered possible to 'grow out' of. By the time the child reaches adolescence and still provokes an IgE histamine reaction to those substances, they are considered to then have that allergy for life and must avoid the substance completely.[23] In contrast, allergies to nuts, seeds, and shellfish are lifelong allergies in the majority of cases and there is no current standard program for developing tolerance to these substances[24] (the peanut allergy test was done on a select group in controlled conditions and is not widely available). So if you are an adult with an allergy, you need to avoid the substance completely.

Wheat allergy versus coeliac disease

For the growing population of people who suffer after eating wheat products, it is important to understand the difference between coeliac disease, wheat allergy and gluten intolerance.

1 in every 100 people suffers with coeliac disease and even then it is thought to be an under-diagnosed condition. Strictly speaking, coeliac disease is not an allergy, it is an autoimmune disorder whereby the body cannot tolerate gluten: the protein found in wheat, barley, rye, and sometimes oats. Symptoms include bloating, diarrhoea, nausea, constipation, tiredness, headaches, hair loss, anaemia and sometimes sudden weight loss. Diagnosis of coeliac disease is via a blood test from your GP followed up with a gut biopsy for confirmation.[25]

Patients with a wheat allergy present with an IgE histamine reaction to wheat alone but not to barley, rye or oats. Wheat allergy is less common than coeliac disease or gluten intolerance.

Gluten intolerance is no less uncomfortable for the patient than coeliac disease but the diagnosis is more difficult. Symptoms are wide-ranging and are typically delayed reactions which are dose dependent. One of the frustrations for those with gluten intolerance versus an allergy or coeliac disease is that patients are sometimes told by GPs that they don't have a problem with gluten if their coeliac test comes back negative. Full information on how you get an intolerance diagnosed is in the next section.

INTOLERANCES

Definition – what is intolerance?

Intolerances are more common than allergies but in general
are much harder to diagnose. They tend to come on slowly and
symptoms can include migraines, lethargy, joint pain, skin problems,
gastrointestinal issues, and more.[1]

Important differences between a food allergy and a food intolerance
include:

1. The symptoms of a food intolerance usually occur several hours
   after eating the food.

2. You generally need to eat a larger amount of food to trigger an
   intolerance than an allergy.

3. A food intolerance is rarely life-threatening, unlike an allergy; the
   reactions are not IgE mediated.[2]

It is possible to be intolerant to any food. However, two of the most
common food intolerances are gluten and dairy.[3]

Prevalence – how many people have intolerances?

Intolerances are a relatively new phenomenon and quoted statistics
on prevalence vary widely. The charity, Allergy UK, has stated that
up to 45% of the population claims to have had a food intolerance
at some point. According to a 2013 survey which illustrates this, 30%
of the American population are now actively trying to avoid gluten.[4]

Restaurants and food manufacturers are responding in turn to consumer demand, and 'free-from' food is now big business. Many health professionals are worried that avoiding wheat or gluten is just another dietary fad, and are concerned that cutting whole food groups out of the diet can lead to malnutrition, especially as gluten-free commercial products are often laden with fats and sugars – not particularly healthy substitutes. Combine this with the fact that intolerance is notoriously difficult to diagnose (medics worry about the 'placebo effect' – you want it to work so it does) and you can understand why doctors are loathe to blame your symptoms on food.

More recently, however, there *has* been acknowledgement from the medical community that wheat, particularly, is an issue for a number of people. The NHS website quotes specialist allergy dietitian at the Royal Brompton and Harefield NHS Foundation Trust, Isabel Skypala PhD, as saying:

'Probably one-third of patients in my allergy clinic complain of digestive symptoms such as bloating, diarrhoea, vomiting and stomach pain after eating bread. Allergy is unlikely to be the culprit, but bread-related symptoms are real and wheat could be to blame. Some people find certain foods are simply hard to digest and wheat appears to be one of those.'[5]

Dairy intolerance, on the other hand, is now quite widely accepted. Lactose intolerance occurs when the body lacks the enzyme lactase, which results in an inability to digest lactose: the sugar component of milk. The lactase enzyme is responsible for breaking the lactose in milk down to glucose and galactose in order for it to be absorbed more easily by the body. If it isn't broken down, the lactose stays in the gut and is fermented by bacteria there, leading to gassiness and bloating in the patient.[6] (Note this is different from a milk allergy, as discussed in the previous section. An allergy to milk is an immune-mediated IgE response to the protein component of milk – whey or casein.)[7]

Prevalence of lactose intolerance varies widely between ethnic groups. For instance, only around 2% people of northern European descent are thought to have lactose intolerance, whereas most people of Chinese descent have it.[8] It is thought that depending on whether we evolved in farming communities where milk consumption was a regular part of the diet or not dictates whether we have evolved to be able to digest milk.[9]

What causes intolerance?

As with allergies, no one is certain what causes food intolerances.

The cause of lactose intolerance is fairly clear cut as the lack of the digestive enzyme, lactase – and you can inherit this condition. Secondary lactose intolerance can also develop after surgery, exposure to certain drugs, or other damage to the functioning of the intestines (e.g. after a bout of gastroenteritis).[10]

In addition, intolerances have generally been linked to erratic dietary habits and poor nutrition with respect to eating highly refined or processed foods.[11] They are also associated strongly with both artificial chemicals in food (such as sulphites and preservatives), and even natural chemicals in food such as caffeine, or histamine found in cheese, chocolate or strawberries.[12]

Diagnosis – elimination diet

Diagnosis of intolerance can be challenging. Currently, the only medically accepted way to diagnose an intolerance is an **elimination diet**, which involves following a limited diet for a number of weeks to allow the gut to heal, followed by reintroducing new foods one at a time and monitoring the patient's reaction to the introduction of individual foods.[13] Intolerances can be dose dependent and after a period of abstinence from the offending food, the patient may find they can tolerate it again (although whether tolerance develops and what quantity is tolerated varies from patient to patient).[14]Understandably, elimination diets are a difficult and time consuming process and patients often therefore look for a definitive test that will point them in the right direction.

Your first point of call if you suspect your medical symptoms may be diet related is always your **GP**. The two main things they can do to test a problem with gluten or dairy are as follows:

1. **Gluten: blood testing for coeliac disease**. This is a simple blood test for particular antibodies (called EMA and tTGA) and positive results are quite conclusive. There are cases of false negative results[15] so blood testing is often followed up by a gut biopsy. In addition, a negative coeliac test does not mean that you aren't still intolerant to gluten; this is often where patients become unstuck when they suspect food intolerances but the doctor says they mustn't have a problem because they aren't coeliac. (If this is you, the best thing to try is an elimination diet – cut gluten out for 4-6 weeks, keep a symptom diary, and if you feel better you can go back to your

doctor with some cause and effect evidence. They may be able to refer you to a dietician if you feel you need some help with healthy eating food plans.)

2. **Lactose intolerance: hydrogen breath test**. This tests for lactose intolerance but results are not always definitive.[16] In addition, you can still be allergic or intolerant to the protein in milk rather than having a problem digesting lactose, so again this is not always conclusive other than to confirm if you have got a lactase deficiency. Interestingly, the hydrogen breath test can also identify those with a problem digesting fructose. Sugar intolerances are a whole other book, but if you suspect this may be you then it is worth speaking to your GP.

Naturopathic practitioners have alternate ways of diagnosing food intolerances and some are more reliable than others (although none have been definitively proven to be effective):

1. **IgG testing** – this is the only testing method for intolerances endorsed by Allergy UK (and some high profile people such as Dr Hilary Jones and Patrick Holford). It involves a blood test for Immunoglobulin G, which is thought to be involved in sensitivity reactions to food. (In other words, IgE is known to be involved in allergies and IgG is thought to be involved with intolerances). There was a high profile study done in 2006 on more than 5,000 patients, of whom 76% reported a marked improvement in their symptoms having eliminated the foodstuffs recommended by IgG testing.[17] Sceptics argued that it wasn't so much that the test was accurate, but

that around 50% of those tested had cut wheat from their diets which is the main culprit in food sensitivity, and that explained why they had an improvement in symptoms.

2. **ALCAT testing** – this is an Antigen Leukocyte Cellular Antibody Test. This is another blood test which examines the reactions of white blood cells to foodstuffs, and is said to diagnose food intolerances which are not mediated by antibodies (such as IgG). This test has not been clinically proven but there is a lot of anecdotal evidence to suggest it is helpful.[18]

3. **Vega testing** – this test measures an electric current applied to acupressure meridians in the body and tests the 'resistance' of your body to different food groups. This type of test is routinely offered in places such as Holland and Barratt, but scientific evidence to prove its efficacy is not forthcoming.[19]

Other methods which are generally discredited by both the scientific community and naturopathic doctors include eye, hair and fingernail analysis, kinesiology, and dowsing (using the movement of a pendulum to 'test' foodstuffs). Please don't waste your money on these!

Food cravings

One interesting indication to be aware of is that you may be intolerant to something if you crave it – this paradoxical symptom is present in about 50% of patients with food intolerances.[20] I can relate to this one myself as I used to eat four bowls of sultana bran cereal with milk every day. I'd feel great for about 30 minutes afterwards and then feel nauseous and lethargic the rest of the time.

Of course, I have an intolerance to both gluten and dairy. This is a well-documented phenomenon in the study of intolerances, so if you are someone who always has cereal and milk for breakfast, a cheese sandwich for lunch and a milky drink and biscuits before bed, then dairy and gluten could be the culprits.

Treatment – what should I do if I think I am intolerant?

Your first port of call should be your GP for a coeliac test and a hydrogen breath test (you may need a referral for the hydrogen breath test, but most surgeries will do the coeliac blood test in-house). If you are diagnosed with lactose intolerance you can take lactase supplements, which will help you to digest dairy products if you do eat them.

It is also imperative that you keep a symptom and food diary for at least a two week period (ideally longer) as this will help you to identify which foods you think are causing you a problem, and will give your GP something to start with. It is important to remember that any foods can cause an intolerance (not just gluten and dairy) and that your symptoms may not be food related at all – you may have other medical issues which need addressing.

There has been progress in recent years in terms of food intolerances being accepted by the medical community; for instance, it is now widely acknowledged that foods such as chocolate, cheese, red wine and citrus fruit can trigger migraines.[21] There is also a diet that NHS consultants are currently recommending to patients with irritable bowel syndrome called the anti-bloat or FODMAP diet. This involves cutting out wheat, milk, and some fermentable foods such as onion, apple, pears, mushrooms, honey and cabbage. The diet must be supervised by a dietician and it has proved effective for 70% of IBS patients.[22,23] If your main intolerance symptoms are IBS related then it is definitely worth seeing your GP about this diet. It is stricter than a simply gluten and dairy-free diet but it does get results.

The best advice I have been given so far by a medical professional is to **'keep a symptom diary and listen to your body.'** By keeping a diary of what you have eaten each day and how it made you feel not only at the time but also afterwards, you will become attuned to what suits your body and what doesn't. This is such an easy thing to do and can take as little as five minutes a day just to write down what you ate and how you felt. Trust your instinct and what your body is telling you; if it doesn't make you feel good, don't eat it!

The healing crisis
Naturopaths caution that those following an elimination diet (i.e. cutting out the foods suspected of causing intolerances) can experience what is called a 'healing crisis', which is a exacerbated level of symptoms for a period of time while the body readjusts and eliminates toxins.[24] Many naturopaths positively welcome the onset of this increased level of symptoms in their patients as they recognise that this is the body's first step in the healing process. This is another reason that elimination diets should really be monitored by a healthcare professional.

Long term
With regard to intolerance, the most important thing to remember is to generally follow a healthy, varied and balanced diet. Cutting

out gluten and/or dairy but adding in fat-laden or sugary foods to compensate in the form of gluten-free biscuits and cakes is not going to improve your health in the long term. *Healthy* gluten and dairy-free eating can be a significant lifestyle change; this book is designed to help you make that change as easy as possible.

Once you have identified the cause of your intolerance and adapted your diet to eliminate the offending food(s) for a period of 4-8 weeks, this will help your body to build up a 'tolerance' to that food.[25] Most people find that after avoiding the food for a while, they can then start to add the food back into their diet – how much of the food can be added back in varies between individuals, and symptom recurrence can be dose dependent, so you need to figure out what works for you and get in tune with what your body tells you.

In summary:

- For **allergy sufferers** – treatment is to avoid the food for life. Carry an EpiPen

- For **allergy sufferers to gluten, dairy, egg and soya** – it is possible for children to grow out of these allergies. See an allergy specialist who can advise a treatment program to try and develop tolerance to the offending food. As an adult, it is unlikely for you to outgrow the allergy so treatment is to avoid the offending food

- For those with **intolerances** – keep a symptom diary for 2-4 weeks to identify the offending foods. Speak to your GP armed with some evidence of which foods are causing you an issue, and discuss diagnostic measures such as elimination diets and hydrogen breath testing, or the possibility of referral to a dietician. Once you have identified which foods are causing you an issue, avoid them for a period of 4-8 weeks before slowly trying to reintroduce them

- For **coeliacs** – get a blood test from your doctor and a firm diagnosis. Avoid gluten for life. Follow a healthy diet

- I have personally found **naturopathic practitioners** to be excellent value for money. IgG intolerance testing, while not definitive or clinically proven, can certainly be helpful to point you in the right direction and cross reference against food diaries. Naturopathic practitioners also offer a plethora of helpful dietary information, and longer appointment times means they can take a much more holistic approach

- It is important that you speak to a **medical practitioner** for a diagnosis and proper dietary advice before you do embark on any self-therapy. Symptoms you are experiencing may not be diet related and it is important to rule out any underlying conditions

PART TWO: HEALTHY EATING – FREE-FROM AND HEALTHY MADE EASY

One of the important things to accept if you suffer with food allergies or intolerances is that you are undoubtedly 'sensitive'. As we discussed in the last chapter, food intolerances are strongly correlated with unhealthy diets high in processed and refined foods.[1] As such, we need to be very careful what we put in our bodies.

For me, combining free-from *and* healthy eating was one of the most difficult things to come to terms with about my food intolerances. I am a classic 'eat on the go' kind of person, with lots to do and never enough time to do it. Planning meals did not feature in my schedule and I would invariably grab the nearest thing to eat when I got hungry (sandwich and crisps on a meal deal at lunch sound familiar to anyone?).

This next section talks about healthy eating guidelines and how to be healthy (and feel great!) when eating 'free-from'. I've started below with my top ten tips for healthy eating – most are quick and easy to implement.

Top ten tips for healthy eating

1. Don't skip breakfast. As I am sure you have heard before, breakfast is the most important meal of the day – it kick starts your metabolism and sets you up for the day. Some people who suffer with food intolerances get to the point where they don't even want to eat; they know they are hungry but they can't face the way food makes them feel. Plus, if your intolerance symptoms have you exhausted and running on empty, you may not want to face food first thing. If you are not good in the morning, just grab an apple, banana or some dried fruit on your way out of the door and have it as your 'fix' when you get to work instead of that latte with sugar. Of course, there are also a number of delicious, healthy breakfast options that take very little time to make and there is lots of advice on these in Part Three.

2. Drink water where you can instead of juices, caffeinated products or fizzy drinks. Use filtered water (filters are cheap to buy and the benefit of keeping a jug of filtered water in your fridge is that it will be cold to drink). If water is too boring on its own, try sparkling water with a slice of lemon. Hot water instead of tea or coffee with a slice of lemon and root ginger is lovely. You can add a number of healthy things to water: have it cold with citrus fruits like limes or oranges or warm with honey, mint or any number of herbal teas.

3. Go organic – particularly with meat products. It is common practice in the food industry to fatten animals up using wheat grains, hormones and by giving them routine antibiotics. Non-organic meat often has chemical additives as well.[2] For those with food sensitivities, it is a sensible idea to limit your exposure to chemicals and antibiotics so look for organic meats that have been grass-fed. A joint study in 2009 by the United States Department of Agriculture and researchers at Clemson University in South Carolina compared grass-fed and grain-fed beef. They found the grass-fed beef to be higher in vitamins and minerals (288% higher in vitamin E and 193% higher in omega 3) and lower in total fat content.[3]

Also switch to organic free-range eggs for a higher omega 3 content. Omega 3 is an essential fatty acid that our bodies don't produce (we need to get it from our diet) and it is known for its anti-inflammatory properties[4] (and for those with food allergies or intolerances, an anti-inflammatory effect is definitely what we are looking for – more on this later).

4. Wash fruit and vegetables properly, especially if they are non-organic, in order to remove pesticides; there is a suggested causal link between pesticides in food and the development of allergies.[5] The skin of fruits and vegetables often has the highest nutritional value so it is not always necessary to peel them as long as they are washed thoroughly. In general, fruit with a more permeable skin (berries, for example) will have a higher pesticide residue; for fruit like this you should ideally buy organic. Another way to reduce pesticide consumption is to soak non-organic fruit in water with a splash of apple cider vinegar and rinse before eating (don't worry, you won't taste the vinegar once the fruit is rinsed). You can check out the Environmental Working Group's website www.ewg.org to see their lists of the most and least pesticide ridden produce.[6]

5. Beware of sugar. Fat used to be thought of as the main culprit in unhealthy lifestyles, but more and more studies are now showing that sugar overload is equally dangerous. Use natural sweeteners such as honey or maple syrup where possible (e.g. in breakfast porridge or even in tea). Try to avoid artificial sweeteners and use natural products like xylitol or stevia (brand name Canderel) if you do use them – these are plant based products and better for you than chemicals such as aspartame. If you do have sugar in your tea or coffee then choose either stevia or natural sugar (wean yourself down to three-quarters of a spoonful rather than one spoonful – every little helps!).

6. Understand fat. There is currently a huge debate raging between scientists regarding recent research which says that saturated fats are not as bad as we once thought they were, and that overconsumption of omega 6 fats such as sunflower oil or corn oil (which we were once told were good for us) can cause inflammation in the body in excessive doses.[7,8] Processed foods such as cakes, biscuits, French fries and crisps often contain high levels of omega 6 rich vegetable oils, which is one of the reasons we should avoid those foods as well as avoiding cooking with those oils. One of the other reasons to avoid cooking with vegetable oils is that they generally have a low smoke point and can oxidise easily, producing harmful free-radicals at high temperatures.[9]

The most recent recommendations are to go back to cooking with 'natural' substances that are solid at room temperature like butter or ghee. For those with dairy allergies, you can cook with coconut oil, palm oil, lard or tallow. (If you don't like the taste of coconut oil you could try refined coconut oil which is mild tasting.)

Olive oil does have a slightly higher burn point than vegetable oils so if you are not using coconut oil then olive oil is at least better than vegetable oils for cooking. Olive and canola (rapeseed) oil are high in omega 9 content and are good, healthy choices for salads when they aren't heated.[10]

7. Eat a variety of foods and remember that the more colourful your plate the better – it is said the more red, green and purple foods we eat, the healthier we will be. Have a policy each meal time of 'at least one fruit or veg' to try and fulfil your five-a-day requirements. You can add one extra fruit or vegetable per week that you wouldn't normally eat to your weekly shopping list. The antioxidants contained in fruit and vegetables help the immune system; again this is very important for those with allergies or intolerances.

8. Eat whole foods. Avoid processed foods at all costs. Don't go gluten and dairy free and then pump your body full of the chemicals contained in processed foods; these are known to be a problem for those with intolerances and sensitivities. It is a mistake to think that because a product is gluten free or dairy free it is healthy for you – despite what manufacturers try to promote. (This also applies to diet foods which often take the fat out of products but add sugar instead.) Also, processed or preserved meats are not good for you; things like ham, gammon, salami or smoked foods. Look for nitrate-free products and choose non-smoked meats. Even dried fruit can be preserved with sulphites which are a well-known allergen – check your food labels carefully.

9. Prepare your food well. Steam vegetables rather than boiling them to retain the nutrients. You can buy stainless steel vegetable steamers that go in your saucepans and reuse the nutrient-dense water when you make gravy or stews. **Grill or bake food** if possible rather than frying. **Limit your acrylamide intake by not burning food**. Acrylamide is a chemical that is produced by starchy foods which are cooked at high temperatures (e.g. French fries) and it has been shown to cause cancer in animals.[11] Potatoes produce less acrylamide if stored in a cupboard rather than the fridge, and less will also be produced if chips are cooked to a lighter rather than a darker colour.

10. Consider supplements. People with food intolerances and allergies can be at risk of missing out on a number of nutrients if they are not conscientious about following a varied diet. Things to consider include calcium supplements on a dairy restricted diet, omega 3 to reduce inflammation, probiotics to heal the digestive system and antioxidants to boost the immune system. More advice on this under the supplements section.

A BALANCED DIET

W hich foods we should be eating in which proportions has long been debated. I have had experience of a number of different dietary recommendations over the years including the 'Eatwell Plate' of the British Dietetic Association, the low GI diet, Atkins diet, the 5:2 diet, to the most recent press coverage of the Paleo diet. Each diet does have something to recommend itself, for instance:

The Low GI diet – GI stands for glycaemic index, and the idea with this is that you need to concentrate on eating foods that promote a slower release of insulin into the system and don't give you an immediate sugar rush – this helps to balance out your blood sugar levels during the day and leads to fewer food cravings. For example, high GI foods that you should limit include things like white bread, baked potatoes, cornflakes and watermelon. Low GI foods which you want to eat more of are things like peanuts, meat, oats and whole grains. The idea is that if high levels of glucose enter the bloodstream on a regular basis, the body quickly converts this glucose to storage fat as it sees it as excess energy, and this can lead to weight gain. In addition, it is said that regular high sugar load promotes insulin resistance and can lead to conditions such as Type 2 Diabetes.[12]

The Atkins diet – Popular in the nineties and the scrutiny of much debate, Dr Robert Atkins recommended that we cut carbs completely from our diet to improve weight loss. For those on a gluten-free diet, this may seem like a great idea, but Dr Atkins came under fire for promoting too much protein and saturated fat in his diet and not enough fruits and vegetables (interestingly, the promoters of the Atkins diet have recently changed some of their recommendations to include more vegetables).[13]

5:2 diet – this diet was popularised by Dr Michael Moseley and looks at research which suggests that those on limited calorie intakes live longer. He says instead of feeling miserable by limiting our calorie intake every day, you should limit your calories on two days per week to about quarter of your normal intake. This helps weight loss which ultimately promotes longevity and also gives the body a digestive break and time to recuperate.[14] Related to this idea is another recent study published in the British Medical Journal which has shown that not eating late in the evening and therefore leaving a 12 hour fasting gap each day can help to promote weight loss (for instance, don't eat between 7pm and 7am).[15]

The Paleo Diet has been popular in the last 2-3 years and it recommends that we eat like our ancestors (Palaeolithic man) did; if the caveman didn't eat it, we shouldn't either. Paleo recommends no processed foods, carbohydrates, legumes (beans, lentils, peas), refined sugar or dairy. It recommends eating meat, fish, vegetables, fruits, nuts and seeds. This is a great diet for those with gluten and dairy problems.[16]

The 'Eatwell Plate' of the British Dietetic Association – the UK's official dietary guidelines; they are what I learned at University and are generally still the recommended guidelines taught to healthcare professionals. Recommendations include the following: five portions of fruit and vegetables a day, three portions of calcium rich food (like dairy) a day, two portions of protein such as meat, fish, or beans a day, and two portions per week of oily fish (such as salmon, sardines, mackerel, herring) with a high omega 3 content. The guidelines state that around 30% of your calories should come from carbohydrates, 30% from fruit and vegetables, 15% from protein, 15% from dairy and less than 10% should be made up of 'treats' in the form of foods high in fat and sugar.[17]

My preferred balance is a 2011 published guide to healthy eating by **Harvard Medical School**, which I think takes the best of the above dietary recommendations and works well for a dairy and gluten-free lifestyle. It recommends that **50% of your calories should come from fruit and vegetables, 25% from 'healthy protein' and 25% from whole grains (such as brown rice, quinoa, oats). Other advice is to avoid sugary drinks, limit dairy, avoid unhealthy protein like processed meats, and use healthy oils.** [18]

One last thing to bear in mind with respect to healthy eating recommendations is that there are numerous studies which show that fat intake can actually be good for you. The key here, of course is the type of fat you are eating; so omega 3 fat from oily fish, eggs and even organic animal meats, and omega 9 fats from avocados and olive oil are GOOD fats. Eating some fat with every meal means you are sated; you won't get the sugar highs and lows from eating too many carbs and are likely to then eat fewer calories.[19]

What to buy

Reading labels in the supermarket has long been my nemesis (particularly if you are trying to do it with toddlers underfoot!).

You would think you need a PhD in Nutrition Science to get your head around some of the things our foods contain, and it seems the vast majority of processed foods do contain some type of milk or gluten product. Allergens like milk and gluten now have to be labelled in bold on packaging, so as long as you are aware and read the label carefully, you can normally avoid the offending item(s).

For a number of reasons, therefore, it is important to eat non-processed whole foods. The following section tells you what you look for when you are buying dairy and gluten free and also gives you a list of free-from foods to keep in stock.

Gluten

When going gluten free you will need to avoid **wheat, barley, rye and sometimes oats** (unless they are specifically labelled gluten free). In general, this means cutting out bread and pasta and replacing it with gluten-free substitutes, as well as incorporating other starchy carbohydrates (such as potatoes, rice, lentils or beans).

Other names you may come across on labels which mean there is gluten contained in the product are as follows; **brewer's yeast, bulgur, durum, spelt, graham flour or malt**.

Double check the brand of gluten-free bread you are buying is supplemented with calcium. Also try to buy a brand that is seeded (it is always a good idea to add seeds to the diet where possible as they are full of omega 3s, known for their anti-inflammatory properties.)

Dairy

We all know that dairy products include **milk, yoghurt, cheese and butter**. You must also look out for food ingredient lists that mention **casein, curds, whey or lactose** as these are all components of milk.

When buying dairy-free milk, look for products that don't have any extra additives like sugar or oils. Koko is a good brand of coconut milk and you can also buy unsweetened varieties of almond or hazelnut milk. Other milks include rice milk, oat milk and hemp milk. Be aware if you buy organic brands of dairy-free milk that there is often no added calcium or vitamin D in these, but depending on your particular diet, you may prefer to do this and think about other ways of getting your calcium instead. A 100ml serving of *non*-organic dairy-free milk (e.g. with cereal or porridge) will give you around 15% of your daily calcium. Also be aware that there is a lot of controversy surrounding excessive soya intake,[20,21] so if you are swapping to soya milk, do so with caution or mix it up with other milk or yoghurt substitutes. Soya yoghurts are lovely but for a real cream kick, try coconut yoghurt which is divine! This can be eaten on its own or used to make creamy sauces (note that oat milk is also good for creamy sauces).

Dairy-free spreads are not particularly healthy due to the high content of polyunsaturated fats they contain in the form of vegetable oils. Buy an olive oil dairy-free spread if you have to choose one (e.g. 'Pure Olive' – although this still contains high quantities of vegetable oil as well). Coconut oil, lard, palm oil or tallow are fine for cooking.

Also, you may find if you are intolerant rather than allergic, that you may be able to tolerate organic butter in cooking after a period of abstinence. Often organic, grass-fed butter, particularly when baked in homemade cakes and pastries, is one of the first things that people find they can tolerate when they reintroduce milk.

In addition, those with a lactose intolerance as opposed to an allergy to milk, sometimes also find that they can actually tolerate hard cheeses (the harder the cheese the less lactose it has, so grated parmesan on pasta is a good one to try), or even natural, organic Greek yoghurt (which has very little lactose).[22]

Finally, you can look out for dairy-free cheeses in specialist stores and it is also now possible to buy lactase fortified dairy products (e.g. Lactaid) like milk, cheese and ice cream. For those with a lactose intolerance rather than milk allergy, it may be useful to consider either buying these products or taking lactase digestive enzyme supplements with any meals containing dairy.

The following is a list of things to keep in your cupboard – all of which you will need for the recipes in this book.

Suitable dairy-free and gluten-free foods for your cupboard

- Salt. Use rock salt or you can also buy a salt with seaweed combination (seaweed contains calcium as well as a number of other minerals) that I use on scrambled eggs or mashed potatoes. One brand you can get from the health food shop is called Seagreens 'Mineral Salt'

- Pepper

- Herb supply – fresh is always best but otherwise frozen is good, or even dried: bay leaf, basil, cinnamon, cumin, coriander, lemon grass, parsley, paprika, rosemary, thyme, mixed herbs, etc.

- Chilli

- Ginger

- Garlic

- Lemon (freeze the lemon and grate the zest. Wash well. Lemon peel has far more vitamins than the rest of the lemon)

- Honey (locally sourced honey is good for those suffering with pollen allergies)

- Maple syrup

- Sugar free jam – look for fruit jams with no added sugar

- Full fat Hellman's mayonnaise (the low fat variety contains milk)

- Salad cream

- Seafood sauce (check brands – Kraft Thousand Island dressing is fine)

- Heinz reduced salt and sugar ketchup

- Tamari soy sauce (this is gluten-free soy sauce and is delicious!)

- Fish sauce

- Apple cider vinegar

- Gluten-free stock cubes

- Gluten-free gravy granules

- Gravy browning

- Gluten-free flour

- Gluten-free breadcrumbs

- Cornflour

- Baking powder

- Dried fruit such as apricots, cranberries or mango – check labels for no added sugars or preservatives (e.g. sulphites)

- Nuts – such as peanuts, cashew nuts, almonds

- Seeds – such as pumpkin, sunflower, flaxseeds, sesame seeds

- Organic, dark, dairy-free chocolate (for cooking with especially) containing a high % of cocoa

- Organic tinned tomatoes, tomato paste and passata

- Pasta sauces (the Seeds of Change organic brand is a

good one)

- Balsamic vinegar

- Olive oil, avocado oil or canola (rapeseed) oil for salads

- Coconut oil to cook

- Sauerkraut (this is a lacto fermented vegetable and contains natural probiotics)

- Miso paste (again contains probiotics)

- Rice noodles or gluten-free corn or rice pasta

- Risotto rice

- Brown rice (vacuum packed brown rice with nothing added which cooks in 2 minutes)

- Gluten-free seeded bread

- Lentils (again the vacuum packed ones are handy)

- Quinoa

- Rice cakes

- Popping corn

- Eggs – organic free-range

- Tinned tuna

- Tinned salmon

- Baked beans (reduced sugar and salt or try the five bean variety)

- Kidney beans

- Chick peas

- Borlotti beans

- Cannellini beans

Things to keep in your freezer

- Spare gluten-free milk and bread in case you run out

- Lemon – can grate this for zest when required

- Fresh ginger to grate

- Frozen herbs

- Spinach – frozen cubes of organic cooked spinach for adding to recipes (great way of sneaking in lots of vitamins)

- Peas, sweetcorn, brussels sprouts and other frozen steam vegetable packs (frozen vegetables have often retained more nutrients than fresh ones which have been kept for too long. Frozen sweetcorn contains nearly double the nutrients of tinned sweetcorn)

- Steamed rice and vegetable packs – great for a quick and easy snack

- Fruit lollies (you can buy natural fruit lollies or make your own by simply buying fresh juices and pouring into ice lolly moulds (never buy juice from concentrate – the manufacturing process has removed most of the nutrients and they typically have a lot of added sugar)

- Frozen fruit such as strawberries, bananas, raspberries or blueberries – handy for making homemade smoothies

Buy your meat, fruit, and vegetables fresh and organic if possible. Choose as much of a variety as you can when it comes to fruit and vegetables; make it an aim to try at least one new fruit or vegetable a week.

SUPPLEMENTS

Accepted wisdom is that vitamin and mineral supplements are not necessary as long as we eat a varied and balanced diet. As a pharmacist (and therefore long time vitamin seller), we professionally subscribe to the above theory that if you are eating healthily you don't need supplements. In fact, the people we see in pharmacies buying multi-vitamins are typically the ones who don't need them: if you are health conscious enough to buy vitamins, you are probably health conscious enough to eat a balanced diet already.

However, one of the dangers of going gluten and dairy free is that if you replace gluten and dairy with other foods which aren't healthy, not only will you not feel better, but you are putting your body at risk of being deficient in nutrients such as calcium (in the case of dairy) and fibre (in the case of gluten).

In addition to this, there are a few supplements which do carry scientific weight regarding their health benefits. Let's start with omega 3:

Omega 3
Numerous studies have shown the health benefits of omega 3 oils on inflammatory conditions including reducing systolic blood pressure, improving circulation, reducing blood triglycerides, and there are also some preliminary findings for proof it helps rheumatoid arthritis.[1] Evidence of their clinical efficacy is strong in these settings and further studies are being conducted on their use in helping patients

with other conditions such as bowel disease, asthma and eczema, although evidence here is not yet as strong.[2]

The best way to get enough omega 3 oils is to eat two portions of oily fish per week; this includes mackerel, salmon, sardines, anchovies, herring, and tuna (not tinned tuna, tuna steaks). Flaxseeds, chia seeds and walnuts are also a good source of omega 3 (you can buy flaxseeds from the health food store and sprinkle over your food – e.g. morning porridge). Vegetable sources of omega 3s include kale, brussels sprouts, spinach, and cabbage. Organic, grass-fed animals are also a source of omega 3 (grain-fed animals less so) as are eggs from organically fed, free-range hens. Indeed, a joint study by the USDA and researchers at Clemson University in South Carolina, found that fat from organically reared, grass-fed animals contained 193% more omega 3 than grain-fed, non-organic animals.[3]

Official British Dietetic Association recommendations are for two portions of oily fish per week for women and four portions for men. This is because of pollutants such as mercury and dioxins in fish which at high levels can be toxic (particularly for unborn foetuses, which is why the recommended limits for women are lower). As the benefits of omega 3 can be outweighed by the toxins in fish (again, everything in moderation!), it may actually be more beneficial to take an omega 3 supplement rather than overdose on oily fish.[4]

There are also two other omega oils to take into consideration: omega 6 and omega 9. Omega 3 and 6 are the oils that the body cannot manufacture on its own – we need to get these from our diet. Omega 9 (e.g. in avocados, olive oil or rapeseed/ canola oil) can be made by the body so is still important, but not as essential as omega 3 and 6.

Historically, when human beings existed on the 'Palaeolithic diet' (of grass-fed meat, nuts, seeds, fruits and berries) we ate omega 3 and omega 6 oils in a roughly 1:1 ratio. Nowadays, because so many omega 6 vegetable oils are being used in processed foods (such as biscuits, cakes and crisps), the average western diet consists of an omega 3:6 ratio of more like 1:16 rather than 1:1. This is not healthy for us. Indeed, recent studies have now shown that chronic, excessive consumption of omega 6 oil versus our omega 3 intake can lead to a number of inflammatory conditions such as arthritis and cancer.[6] We need therefore to reduce our intake of omega 6 oils (like sunflower oil) and increase our intake of omega 3 oils (found in oily fish). I know this sounds surprising when for years we have been told that plant oils (such as corn or sunflower oil) are healthy.

It is important to make sure you buy a good quality supplement (ask your local pharmacist) and also to be careful of the liquid supplements which can easily oxidise (go rancid) when exposed to air. A dose of 500-1000mg per day is recommended.[5]

Fat in general is a confusing subject, and in recent times our thoughts have also been completely turned around regarding the recommended intake of saturated fat. We had been told for years that animal fat is bad for us as it contains a lot of saturated fat (as does butter, lard, ghee and coconut oil). Studies showing saturated fat linked to heart disease and promoting instead the consumption of vegetable oils have been accepted by the general public for at least

50 years. However, in recent times, large scale studies have disproved this theory of saturated fat making us fat and some studies even point to the fact that the opposite is true.[7,8]

The British Heart Foundation and the British Dietetic Association still do not recommend eating saturated fat for its health benefits but do now universally acknowledge that saturated fat is not the demon we once thought it was.

Olive oil, rapeseed oil (canola) and avocado oil are high in omega 9 content and are generally recommended as healthy oils to eat cold (as salad dressing for example). However, you do need to be careful when heating these oils as they can oxidise at high temperatures, producing harmful free-radicals. Olive oil oxidises less readily than vegetable oils, but there is now mounting evidence to suggest that using a natural oil such as coconut oil for cooking is more beneficial for health.[9] Fats such as coconut oil, lard or tallow are solid at room temperature (as are butter and ghee but these are not dairy-free) so take longer to reach the high temperatures required for oxidation and the production of harmful free-radicals.

Bottom line on fats:

- Eat lots of omega 3 – ideally two portions of oily fish a week, or else take a supplement

- Eat less omega 6 – these are vegetable oils like corn or sunflower oil found in processed goods such as cakes, biscuits, crisps. Don't cook with vegetable oils as not only does this increase your omega 6 intake, but these oils oxidise easily producing free-radicals at high temperatures

- Use omega 9 rich olive oil or rapeseed/canola oil as dressings and on cold food

- Don't be scared of saturated fat anymore, particularly when it comes from natural sources like organic meat or coconut oil. Fat intake in the diet is satiating and prevents you overloading on other food groups such as sugars and carbohydrates.[10] Remember, everything in balance!

Probiotics

Probiotics have become increasingly popular in the last decade. Companies selling brands such as Yakult and Actimel yoghurt drinks heavily promote the idea that our tummies need 'good bacteria' in order to be healthy.

One of the difficulties with these yoghurt drinks (apart from the fact that those with a dairy sensitivity cannot take them) is that they are also loaded with sugar (not healthy!) and only a few brands contain anything like the level of live bacteria required to have a beneficial clinical effect.

However, there is truth in the premise of 'good bacteria' and the need to establish a healthy intestinal gut flora. The theory behind the use of probiotics goes back to the hygiene hypothesis we discussed in the first chapter. Overuse of antibiotics or even a bout of gastroenteritis can lead to the 'good' bacteria being stripped from the intestinal flora. Medics think that this is one of the things that has led to the rise in allergies and food sensitivities.[1]

Probiotics are currently actively used in the treatment of antibiotic associated diarrhoea.[2] There are also trials showing positive outcomes for patients with irritable bowel syndrome and lactose intolerance. (It is thought the lactase enzyme produced by the bacteria helps lactose intolerant patients digest milk more easily).[3,4]

Probiotic supplements can be expensive (£25 for a month's course) and it is recommended to make sure the product you are buying is live and contains at least 10 billion CFU (colony forming units – this denotes the strength of the product). It is also a good idea to vary which probiotic formula you take as different formulas contain different types of bacteria, and you want a good mix of around five or six different strains. If you take both a high strength and multi-bacterial probiotic daily for around a month you should have colonised your gut sufficiently to then reduce your weekly quantity of probiotic (say to around twice a week, but check your specific circumstances with your healthcare professional). Also, double check that the supplement you get does not contain lactose as a filler or any other dairy containing products.

Lactic acid fermented foods (also known as lacto-fermented-enzyme-enhanced foods) such as sauerkraut, dill pickles, miso paste or tamari sauce naturally contain probiotic bacteria. It is a good idea to add these foods to your diet where you can.

Bottom line on probiotics:
- Probiotics are good for your digestive health and clinical evidence of their efficacy is mounting

- Take a supplement (check it is a high strength, good quality one) and include probiotic containing foods (such as miso soup, sauerkraut, or tamari sauce) in your diet

Calcium and vitamin D

Those following dairy-free diets must be careful to ensure that levels of calcium intake are adequate. Calcium is important for maintaining strong bones, muscles, and nerves and is required for blood vessels to operate properly so that enzymes can break down our food. Osteoporosis is caused by calcium deficiency, and is so common in the UK now that one in three women and one in six men is likely to suffer an osteoporotic fracture. Calcium absorption is helped by vitamin D, otherwise known as the 'sunshine' vitamin as the body produces vitamin D in response to sunlight. One interesting fact is that children with a vitamin D deficiency (for example those born in the autumn time when there is less sunlight), have a higher prevalence of allergies.[1]

As a rule of thumb adults need 700mg of calcium per day, children under 10 need 500mg per day and adolescents need 1000mg per day. Full requirements according to the British Dietetic Association are as follows:

Group	Age (years)	Calcium (mg) per day	No.of Calcium stars
Adults	19+	700mg	11 stars
Adoles-cents	11-18	800mg girls	13 stars
		1000mg boys	16 stars
Children	1-3	350mg	6 stars
	4-6	450mg	7.5 stars
	7-10	550mg	9 stars
Infants	Under 1	525mg	9 stars

Foods other than milk which contain calcium include:

Food	Stars
Calcium enriched orange juice (250ml)	***
Calcium enriched soya, rice, or oat milk (200ml)	***
Calcium fortified cereals/porridge oats (check packages) (one serving)	* to ***
Calcium fortified soya yoghurt/dessert custard	**
Sardines (60g or half a tin)	****
Baked beans (small tin, 220g)	***
Tinned salmon (half a tin)	*
Bread (two slices)	*
Spinach (one boiled serving 120g)	***
Fig (four dried)	***
Hummus (one serving 150g)	**
Broccoli	*
Spring greens	*
Brazil nuts – nine (30g)	*
Almonds (30g)	*
Orange – one	*
Apricots	*
Tofu (100g)	***

2

So for an adult to have enough calcium for the day, they need 11 stars. This could consist of: for breakfast, a calcium fortified cereal, with calcium fortified oat/rice/almond milk plus soya yoghurt with a glass of calcium fortified orange juice. Add in salmon sandwiches for lunch with a handful of apricots or almonds, and not only have you ticked off your calcium requirements but also part of your weekly omega 3 intake.

It is worth paying attention to which brands of products you buy and also taking care to read the labels. There is some controversy about fortified foods not being 'natural', and the healthiest approach would certainly be to focus on eating more spinach, almonds and figs than to try and supplement calcium through fortified foods or supplements. Part of the reason for this controversy (apart from the fact that natural, non-processed foods are best) is the bioavailability of calcium in supplements and fortified products (i.e. how well it is absorbed by the body). To maximise absorption of calcium, it is important to take it with a vitamin D supplement as well as taking it with food (this slows transit time through the gut and allows the calcium time to be absorbed). Also, be aware that foods high in iron (e.g. beef, beans or dark leafy greens) can reduce how well calcium is absorbed.

My practical standpoint is that if you are not a big fan of figs and sardines and worry that your calcium levels are low, it is worthwhile thinking about a supplement. Make sure you take a supplement that contains both calcium and vitamin D. A reasonable daily dose is around 500mg-800mg and do bear in mind that it *is* possible to overdose on calcium supplements. Excessively high calcium levels can lead to impaired kidney function as well as decreased absorption of other minerals such as iron, zinc and magnesium. There have also been studies to show that calcium supplementation can lead to cardiovascular problems and an increased risk of heart attacks.[3,4]

Bottom line on calcium and vitamin D:

- Try to incorporate calcium containing foods into your diet on a daily basis

- If you think you are not eating enough calcium as specified above then you may want to consider taking a calcium and vitamin D supplement. Take around 500mg-800mg daily and take it with food to help absorption

- Remember you can overdose on calcium supplements so by far the best way to get enough calcium is through your diet

Digestive enzymes

For those with intolerances rather than allergies, digestive enzyme supplements are widely promoted and a couple of them are known to be helpful and effective.

Lactase

Lactase is the enzyme that breaks lactose (the sugar component of milk) down into its constituent molecules, glucose and galactose, to enable absorption by the body. A lack of the lactase enzyme means that lactose stays in the gut and is fermented by bacteria there, leading to gassiness and bloating in the patient. Supplementing with lactase absolutely does help the body to digest lactose properly, so trying a product like Lactaid when you drink milk can help those with lactose intolerance to digest it better. The key of course is to have a diagnosis of lactose intolerance; those with milk allergies will not be helped by lactase supplements.

Beano

Beano contains the enzyme alpha galactosidase which works in the digestive tract to break down complex sugars in certain foods into simple sugars which can be more easily absorbed by the body. Foods such as beans, cauliflower, broccoli, cabbage and brussels sprouts can ferment in the gut if not broken down properly and Beano has been proven in clinical trials to relieve the symptoms this causes such as gas, bloating and discomfort.[1,2]

How you eat is important too
In addition, on a more practical note, naturopathic practitioners often counsel on the importance of *how* you eat your meal. Taking time to chew your food properly can have a big impact on how well you digest it. As can allowing your olfactory senses to become stimulated as you prepare your meal; we all know the sensation of the smell of good food making us salivate, this anticipation also stimulates the gut to release digestive enzymes. So do as your mother told you; take your time to eat and don't gulp your food down!

Fibre

The main danger we are warned about when going gluten free is the lack of fibre in our diet. There are two different types of fibre: soluble and insoluble. Soluble fibre is found in foods such as oats, nuts, seeds, certain fruits and legumes. Soluble fibre slows down digestion and helps to lower blood cholesterol levels. Insoluble fibre is found in foods such as wheat bran, barley, brown rice, quinoa and vegetables such as celery, broccoli, onions and cabbage. Insoluble fibre is important to regulate bowel function and prevent constipation.

The wheat bran in bread can be an important source of fibre for many. However, bread only contains 1.3g of fibre per slice compared with 3.2g in muesli, 1.3g in porridge, 2.6g in broccoli, 1.8g in an apple or 1.2g in a banana.[1]

Further, it used to be argued that gluten-free products were not fortified with vitamins and minerals such as calcium, iron or B vitamins as are most commercially produced breads. Bread is never to be considered a 'health food' due to the heavy processing and manufacturing it undergoes, but nowadays nearly all gluten-free breads are fortified with the same vitamins as normal varieties, so this is no longer an issue.

Bottom line on fibre:

- Fibre is an important part of a healthy diet

- On a gluten-free diet you shouldn't need to supplement with fibre other than making sure you eat lots of fruit, vegetables, brown rice and porridge. Buy gluten-free bread that is brown, seeded and fortified with vitamins

- Bread is not a crucial part of a healthy diet so stop worrying that you are not getting enough fibre if you don't get it from bread. Focus on ensuring the other carbohydrates you eat are healthy

- If you feel you aren't eating enough fibre containing foods then it is possible to supplement with a dietary fibre called psyllium; ask at your pharmacy or health food shop

Antioxidants

Foods that are rich in antioxidants (such as vitamins A,C and E plus selenium and zinc) help to foster a healthy immunity, which is important for those with food allergies and intolerances. A high antioxidant intake has been shown to provide a protective effect on those with allergies and asthma.[1,2]

Try to capture as many foods rich in antioxidants in your diet as possible. A list is below:

Vitamin A: apricots, asparagus, beets, broccoli, cantaloupe, carrots, corn, green peppers, kale, mangoes, turnip and collard greens, nectarines, peaches, pink grapefruit, pumpkin, squash, spinach, sweet potato, tangerines, tomatoes, and watermelon

Vitamin C: berries, broccoli, brussels sprouts, cantaloupe, cauliflower, grapefruit, honeydew, kale, kiwi, lemon, mango, nectarine, orange, papaya, snow peas, sweet potato, strawberries, tomatoes, and red, green, or yellow peppers

Vitamin E: broccoli, carrots, chard, mustard and turnip greens, mangoes, nuts, papaya, pumpkin, red peppers, spinach, and sunflower seeds

Zinc: oysters, red meat, poultry, beans, nuts, seafood, whole grains

Selenium: Brazil nuts, tuna, beef, poultry, whole grains[3]

Tips on getting the most antioxidants from your fruit and vegetables include:

- Steam vegetables rather than boiling to maintain nutrient content

- Wash fruit and vegetables properly to remove pesticides or buy organic

- Eat the skin of the vegetables as this contains the most nutrient content. For instance, when making carrot soup, don't peel the carrots (just top and tail); with jacket potatoes, eat the skin; and use lemon zest from unwaxed lemons where possible in addition to the juice

Bottom line on antioxidants:
For a healthy immune system, make sure you get your five a day!

Food as medicine

Naturopaths treat food as medicine that serves to nourish and heal the body: this is a marvellous philosophy. As well as the foods we discussed above, such as getting enough omega 3 from eating fish, and sufficient antioxidants from fruit and vegetables, I would just like to point out some other foods which are known for their therapeutic effects on the body:

Garlic
Garlic contains vitamin C, vitamin D and manganese. It has been proven in clinical trials to lower blood pressure and cholesterol as well as providing protection to the immune system.[1] I add garlic to most stews I cook not only for the taste but also the health benefits.

Bone broth
Chicken broth for a cold is the natural remedy for all time; there is a reason your mum used to make chicken soup when you were sick.

Bone broth contains numerous minerals like calcium, phosphorus, magnesium and potassium, as well as amino acids like glycine and proline and also collagen. A study conducted by the University of Nebraska Medical Center found that the specific amino acids in bone broth (which aren't normally found in the meat part of the animal) reduced inflammation in the respiratory system and also improved digestion.[2]

Carminatives
Foods such as peppermint, chamomile and ginger are traditional remedies for calming digestive issues. Also try a teaspoon of apple cider vinegar in a glass of water to aid digestion.

Anti-inflammatory foods
There is some controversy about this but foods such as green tea, papaya, blueberries, sweet potato, cocoa, and some spices like ginger and curry are said to be anti-inflammatory.[3]

It is certainly proven that high quantities of omega 6 are pro-inflammatory (e.g. sunflower oil) and omega 3 containing foods (e.g. eggs, nuts, oily fish) are anti-inflammatory. Healthy eating is important for everyone, but those with sensitivity issues should make a conscientious effort to eat more anti-inflammatory foods.

Superfoods
'Superfoods' is a term generally used to describe a foodstuff with supposed health benefits. Dieticians don't officially recognise the term, although the high nutrient density in the following foods is widely acknowledged.[4]

Try to incorporate some of these in your diet every day:

- Goji berries (calcium, potassium, iron, zinc, selenium, vitamin B and vitamin C)

- Green tea (high in antioxidants)

- Berries and citrus fruits (high in antioxidants)

- Spinach (in general green dark leafy vegetables like kale or brussels sprouts – high in iron, calcium and antioxidants)

- Broccoli (vitamin A, B, C, iron, calcium and potassium)

- Avocado (omega 9, potassium, B Vitamins and folic acid)

- Salmon (high in omega 3)

- Sardines (high in omega 3 and calcium)

- Beetroot (high in phytonutrients)

- Sweet potato (vitamin A, C potassium, vitamin B and calcium)

- Nuts and seeds (omega 3 and 6, vitamin B, vitamin E, calcium, iron, fibre, zinc potassium and selenium)

PART THREE: RECIPES

have bought a number of dairy and gluten-free cookbooks in the past in an attempt to come up with ideas to feed my family, and have been overwhelmed by suggestions such as 'stuffed squid with sage and capers', or 'gnocchi with walnut and lemon sauce'. Those aren't practical family meals! I also get overwhelmed with recipes that demand a lot of ingredients. Anything that takes more than 10-15 minutes on a week night and I'm not interested!

This section is designed to appeal to those who, like me, enjoy tasty food but don't like spending ages cooking it; recipes at the beginning of each section are the easiest ones and preparation times are listed for each. The following suggestions are not only tasty, but the recipes also take nutritional requirements into account so they are healthy too. Gluten and dairy free goes without saying, but many recipes are also nut, egg, and soya free too.

BREAKFAST

Breakfast on the Run

Breakfast really is the most important meal of the day and one of the best things you can do to feel healthy is not to skip it. If you are not a 'breakfast person', make an effort to at least grab an apple or a handful of dried apricots on your way out of the door in the morning. Keep a pack of nuts or dried fruit in your bag, car or desk at work so that you have something to nibble on during the day. Even the 'Eat Natural' bars are better than nothing. Be careful what brand of granola bar you buy though as a lot of them are high in sugar.

Porridge Oats

My breakfast of choice is porridge oats; it really is a great breakfast staple. Serve with local honey, maple syrup, no-added-sugar fruit jams or a sprinkle of cinnamon. Add in a handful of fruit; blueberries, raspberries, pomegranate seeds or raisins. You don't need to make porridge with milk if you don't like the taste of dairy-free milks, you can make it with water instead – I do this and actually think it tastes better. If you want your porridge to be as easily digestible as possible, you can soak it overnight in water with half a teaspoon of apple cider vinegar. This releases the phytic acid from the oats and makes them easier to digest, as well as helping with the absorption of vitamins and minerals.[1]

Eggs

Eggs are also a brilliant source of protein and start to the day. For years, eggs had a bad reputation health-wise as they are said to be high in cholesterol. We now know that eggs do not raise cholesterol levels significantly,[2] and (in particular organic free-range eggs which will be higher in omega 3 content) have been called 'the perfect nutrient'[3](after all, they are designed to feed a growing chick). Add some spinach or salmon to your scrambled eggs and you are on to a winner!

Yoghurt and Muesli

Another good choice for breakfast is dairy-free coconut yoghurt or soya yoghurt, both of which are available from either health food stores or supermarkets. Have this with fruit, muesli and some hemp seeds, chia seeds or linseeds/ flaxseeds for an omega 3 morning boost.

Cereal

If you are eating cereal, either Oatibix, Rice Krispies, or cornflakes are wheat free (but note for those with a gluten intolerance or coeliac disease, not barley-free). Oatibix is a reasonable source of fibre, and you can also add blueberries to your bowl and of course serve with dairy-free milk. I would be careful even when choosing gluten-free brands of cereals in supermarkets as they are often still high in sugar content. The other interesting thing to note is that organic ranges of products are also frequently not fortified with vitamins. So, for instance, if you think you are getting a good dose of calcium with your organic rice puffs and organic dairy-free milk then you may well not be unless you check the label of the brand you are buying. It *is* good to buy organic, but you need to weigh that against the level of vitamins you think you are getting overall (particularly calcium on a dairy-free diet) and make a judgement call.

Toast

I am never a big fan of gluten-free bread as it is still a highly processed food. However, if you like toast in the morning, try to buy the brown, seeded variety of gluten-free bread rather than the white stuff, and you can have this with a dairy-free spread or no-added-sugar jam. You could also have peanut, sunflower seed, cashew nut or almond butter on your toast (check brands for no added sugar and no dairy). Top with sliced banana as one of your five a day.

The other great thing to add to toast in the morning for some extra protein is beans or sardines (sardines are packed with calcium and omega 3 oils). This will keep you going longer until lunch. Mackerel on toast with salted cucumber and horseradish is a great zingy start to the day!

Smoothies

Homemade smoothies are another one of my favourites and you can add all kinds of things to them in addition to fruit (e.g. omega 3 oil, coconut yoghurt or avocado). When you get in the habit of making them yourself, it is really quite quick and easy. I keep frozen, ready-chopped fruit in the freezer to defrost for my smoothies. If you are really short on time, no-added-sugar brands of smoothies (like innocent smoothies) are better than having no fruit at all (although eating a piece of fruit is always the preferred option as you have the fibre with it as well).

There are any number of combinations of smoothies and milkshakes you can dream up. Here are a couple of healthy ideas to start:

Milkshake: almond or rice milk, half to one banana, handful of strawberries, flaxseeds

Smoothie: half an avocado, handful of berries, pomegranate juice, handful of spinach leaves, omega 3 supplement oil

MUFFINS

Homemade gluten-free muffins freeze well and are another good grab and go option once you have taken the time to prepare them in the first place.

Banana and Apricot Muffins

Ingredients (makes 12)

- 250g GF flour
- 100g DF spread
- 75g sugar
- 2 large eggs
- ½ tsp baking powder
- ¼ tsp cinnamon
- ¼ tsp nutmeg
- 200g chopped apricots
- 3 ripe bananas

Directions (30 minutes)

Combine the flour, DF spread, sugar, eggs, spices and baking powder together in a bowl and mix well. Mash the bananas and stir them into the mixture along with the chopped apricots. Put into individual muffin cases and bake in the oven at 180 degrees for around 20 minutes or until golden brown.

Raspberry Muffins

Ingredients (makes 12)

- 300g GF flour
- 1 egg
- 75g DF butter
- 100ml DF milk
- 75g sugar
- 75g raspberries
- 2 bananas
- Juice of one lemon
- 2tsp baking powder

Directions (30 minutes)

Whisk the butter, sugar and egg together and sift in the flour and baking powder. Gradually add in the milk, mixing continuously.

Mash the bananas and lemon juice together in a separate bowel until very smooth. Fold the banana mixture and raspberries into the batter. Spoon into muffin cases and bake in the oven for 25 minutes at 160 degrees until golden brown.

SOUPS

The vast majority of store-bought soups contain either gluten or dairy. Store-bought vegetable soups are the least likely to be an issue but always check the labels carefully. Homemade soups are great for batch cooking and freezing and a couple of the recipes below can even be made from scratch in under 10 minutes.

Pea, Ham and Mint Soup

Ingredients (serves 2-3)

- 500ml GF vegetable stock
- Handful of mint leaves
- 500g peas
- 150ml DF milk (I find rice milk or oat milk works best with this one)
- 120 g chopped gammon or ham

Directions (10 minutes)
Heat the stock and add mint leaves and peas, cook for 2 minutes. Strain the mint and peas and put in a blender. Add back in stock, a drizzle of olive oil and rice milk and blend again. Add ham and heat. Season to taste with freshly ground black pepper.

Miso Soup with Rice Noodles

Another quick and easy one. Miso paste is a natural probiotic and great for the digestive system.

Ingredients (serves 1)
- Packaged miso soup paste (Clearspring organic brand is a good one)
- 1 portion rice noodles

Directions (10 minutes)
Cook the noodles by adding boiling water (normally they cook in around 8 minutes). Drain and add to Clearspring soup (making up with the amount of water specified on the pack).

Optional
For additional protein you can add cooked chicken pieces or even an egg to this soup

Carrot and Parsnip Soup

Ingredients (serves 4)

- 5 parsnips, peeled and chopped into large chunks
- 7 carrots, peeled and chopped into large chunks

Directions (15 minutes)

Boil the parsnips and carrots in enough water to cover them. Once cooked, blend the mixture including the water they were cooked in. Add salt and pepper to taste.

Tip

You can also add a GF stock cube to this mixture as well as 1-2 cloves of garlic or half a red chilli to spice it up a bit. If you want it slightly creamier, you can add a bit of oat milk. Use organic vegetables if possible and if doing so, you don't need to peel them, just top and tail; most of the nutrients are contained in the skin so this will retain them. As always, use filtered water rather than tap water when you cover the vegetables and if you have any in the freezer, you can add bone broth to this mixture (see broth recipe).

Tuscan Bean Soup

Ingredients (serves 4-6)

- 3 carrots
- 1 onion
- 1 clove garlic
- 2 celery stalks
- 1 litre GF vegetable stock
- 400g borlotti beans
- 400g kidney beans
- 200g mini GF pasta shapes
- Mixed herbs – oregano and rosemary

Directions (20 minutes)

Cook carrots and pasta. Drain and set aside. Fry onion, garlic and celery then add borlotti and kidney beans to pan to heat through. Add the vegetable stock to the pan then add back in the cooked GF pasta shapes and carrots. Season to taste with oregano and rosemary.

Leek and Potato Soup

Ingredients (serves 3-4)

- 3-4 leeks
- 2 onions
- 5-6 potatoes (slightly larger quantity of potatoes than leeks)
- 150ml DF milk

Directions (25 minutes)

Boil potatoes. Fry leeks and onions in small amount of oil. When potatoes, leeks and onions are cooked, drain potatoes and add all to the same pan. Thin with dairy-free milk (soya or oat milk works well) and blend until mixture is smooth.

Butternut Squash and Autumn Vegetable Soup

This is great as you can get two meals from it. You can roast the following vegetables to accompany a meal and then puree the leftovers to make soup. It is delicious and freezes really well.

Ingredients (serves 8-10)
- 1 aubergine
- 1 butternut squash
- 3-4 sweet potatoes
- 3-4 carrots
- 1 courgette
- 2 red peppers
- 3-4 garlic cloves
- 500ml GF vegetable stock

Directions (30 minutes)

Chop the vegetables into similar sized cubes and roast in the oven along with the whole garlic cloves. Roast on a baking tray in the oven (around 200-220 degrees C) with a reasonable amount of oil. Once cooked, add vegetables to a bowl with 500ml of GF vegetable stock and blend mixture so it is completely smooth. (Note you can add more vegetable stock depending on your preferred consistency).

GO GLUTEN AND DAIRY FREE AND FEEL GREAT!

Lentil and Vegetable Soup

Ingredients (serves 2)

- 1 onion
- 1 carrot
- 1 leek
- 1 potato
- 2 celery sticks
- 50g red lentils
- GF vegetable stock cube
- 1 tbsp GF flour

Directions (40 minutes)

Chop the carrot, leek, potato into similar sized cubes. Dice the onion. Heat oil in a saucepan and fry the vegetables (except potatoes) for 5 minutes. Stir in a tablespoon of flour and cook for 2 minutes. Add a stock cube with 500ml boiling water and bring the pan to the boil. Add the potatoes and red lentils then put a lid on the saucepan and let the ingredients simmer for 30 minutes.

Tip

Depending on the brand, I find with GF stock cubes that you may need a bit more than one stock cube to 500ml of water for sufficient flavour. Add more stock (or other herbs) to taste.

Chicken Broth

This doesn't take more than half an hour to prepare but it does require a 12 hour window between starting the preparation and getting the finished product.

I recommend making this the night after you have cooked a roast chicken. Buy a larger chicken than normal and use the leftover meat for your chicken soup. This recipe is called chicken broth because you will also use the bones from the chicken carcass to make a bone broth, high in minerals such as calcium, phosphorous, magnesium and potassium as well as certain amino acids like glycine and proline that are not found in significant amounts in muscle meat.[5] Bone broths are promoted by naturopaths for healing a leaky gut and are said to improve digestion; they are packed full of vitamins and minerals.[6]

Ingredients

- Whole organic, free-range chicken (grass-fed). Use feet as well if available as these have a lot of cartilage which is what breaks down to collagen
- 1-2 organic carrots – roughly chopped (washed, not peeled)
- 2-3 cloves garlic, crushed
- 1-2 stalks celery, roughly chopped
- GF chicken stock cube
- Filtered water
- 1 tsp apple cider vinegar
- Tin sweetcorn
- Cornflour

Directions for bone broth (30 minutes-12 hours)

88

Take leftover meat from cooked chicken and set aside (put in the fridge overnight). Add chicken carcass to a pan with the chopped onion, celery stalk, garlic and carrot, cover with cold filtered water and add ½-1 tsp of apple cider vinegar (this helps to leach the nutrients from the bones). Leave on a low heat overnight (around 12 hours). The next day strain the liquid away from the chicken and vegetables with a fine mesh sieve. Chill the remaining liquid in the fridge until the fat solidifies and then skim off. You should be left with a gelatinous mixture which will be dense in nutrients and amino acids. This mixture is excellent for healing the digestive system and boosting the immune system. You can warm the broth up and drink it by itself or freeze it to add nutrients to gravy and sauces in cooking. I also like to use it as below in a chicken soup.

Directions for chicken soup
Add a good quantity of bone broth (how much you add depends on taste and how gelatinous you want your soup) to the leftover shredded chicken pieces from above. Throw in some sweetcorn, filtered water and a stock cube and heat. You will love not only the taste but the health benefits as well.

CO GLUTEN AND DAIRY FREE AND FEEL GREAT!

SALADS

Sandwiches and Picky Bits

Sandwiches are standard lunchtime fare and for those with intolerances, overloading on sandwiches may well have been a trigger for the development of a gluten intolerance. If you are having sandwiches at lunch, try to make it more 'salad' than sandwich and keep in mind the following:

1) Add some fruit or vegetables to the side of your plate; my children love this kind of quick food and call it 'picky bits'. I make mini sandwiches but then add to the plate things like: carrot, cucumber or pepper sticks with hummus, cherry tomatoes, slices of fruit or even dried fruit like apricots (full of calcium) or mango.

2) Vary the protein that you have in your sandwich and add some greenery to the sandwich filling. Try tuna crunch or salmon mayonnaise (full fat Hellman's mayonnaise contains no milk) with sweetcorn, diced red pepper and celery plus a squeeze of lemon juice and black pepper. You could also do chicken and avocado, turkey and cranberry with rocket lettuce, egg and cress sandwiches or ham and cucumber. Use gluten-free seeded brown bread.

Easy Peasy Coleslaw

Ingredients (serves 4-6)

- 3 carrots
- ½ head red cabbage
- ½ head green cabbage
- 2 spring onions
- 1 red pepper
- Salad cream

Directions (10 minutes)

Finely chop or grate ingredients, combine together in a bowl. Add salad cream to taste. Serve with a jacket potato.

Colourful Quinoa Salad

I was quite reluctant to eat quinoa for a long time until I realised how versatile and easy it is to cook with. Quinoa is packed full of protein and you can get ready cooked vacuum packed containers which make life really easy. There are lots of different things you can do to dress quinoa up (a bit like different rice salads). A couple of ideas are below:

Ingredients (serves 2)
- 250g quinoa (ready cooked vacuum packed)
- 2 tbsp lemon juice and zest
- 2 tbsp olive oil
- 1 clove garlic
- 1 cm grated ginger root
- 5 radishes, finely chopped
- ¼ cucumber, finely chopped
- ½ red pepper, finely chopped

Directions (10 minutes)
Dice radishes, cucumber and red pepper, add to cooked quinoa. Mix in lemon juice, grated ginger, crushed garlic clove, and olive oil to taste. Serve chilled; this stores well in the fridge and the flavours infuse with keeping.

Optional
If you want a more meaty salad, you can do the same recipe but instead of the ginger, radishes and cucumber, add in tuna, chickpeas and parsley.

Rice Salad

Ingredients (serves 2)

- 250 g rice (the 2 minute microwave pouches of brown rice or quinoa and rice are fine)
- ¼ chopped cucumber
- 10 halved cherry tomatoes
- 3 tbsp sweetcorn
- 120g tuna (approx. one tin)
- Olive oil
- 2 tbsp chopped mini gherkins

Directions (10 minutes)

Cook the rice in the microwave then transfer to the fridge to let it cool down. Chop the cherry tomatoes, gherkins and cucumber into chunks and drizzle in olive oil. When the rice has cooled, stir in the tuna, plus vegetable and oil mix. You may want to add a little cracked black pepper.

Seafood and Avocado Salad

Ingredients (serves 2)

- 100g smoked salmon
- 16 cooked tiger prawns
- 1 ripe avocado
- 100g rocket leaves
- Seafood sauce (most store-bought ones are dairy free or you can make your own using a combination of ketchup plus mayonnaise)

Directions (10 minutes)

Assemble on a plate the rocket leaves, salmon, prawns and slices of avocado. Garnish with seafood sauce, a wedge of lemon and cracked black pepper.

Easy Bean Salad

Ingredients (serves 6)

- 4 spring onions, chopped
- 2 garlic cloves
- 1 red chilli
- 800g cannellini beans, drained and rinsed
- 400g butter beans
- 6 tbsp olive oil
- 2 tbsp apple cider vinegar
- Handful of chopped parsley

Directions (10 minutes)

Finely chop the spring onions and put into a bowl with the garlic and the chilli. Mix in the cannellini beans and the butter beans. Whisk the olive oil with the apple cider vinegar and stir through the salad with chopped parsley.

Tip

This keeps well and is a great side accompaniment to soups or sandwiches – add rocket and make into a salad.

Tomato and Chickpea Salad

Ingredients (serves 2)

- ½ red onion, finely sliced
- 400g chickpeas, drained and rinsed
- 2 large chopped tomatoes
- 2 tbsp lemon juice
- 1 tablespoon olive oil
- Handful of chopped mint and parsley
- Pinch of paprika
- Pinch of ground cumin
- Salt and pepper

Directions (10 minutes)

Simply mix together all the ingredients in a large non-metallic bowl and set aside for 5 minutes to allow the flavours to infuse, then serve.

Herby Lentil Salad with Bacon

Ingredients (serves 2)

- 1 small garlic clove, crushed
- 1 spring onion, sliced
- 300g lentils (either canned or in vacuum sealed pouch is fine)
- 1 tbsp of balsamic vinegar
- 1 tbsp of chopped herbs (such as parsley, oregano or basil)
- 10 cherry tomatoes, halved
- 4 slices of unsmoked back bacon

Directions (15 minutes)

Put a small amount of oil in a pan, add the garlic and spring onion and fry for a minute.

Stir in the lentils, vinegar, herbs and tomatoes and set aside. Grill the bacon until crisp, place on top of the salad and serve.

Tip

If making this salad to eat later, wrap the cooked, crisped bacon in kitchen paper then kitchen foil. Add just before you eat.

Tuna Niçoise Salad

Ingredients (serves 2)

- 100g lettuce (I prefer a rocket and spinach mix – full of calcium again – but any will do)
- 10 olives
- 6 anchovies (the ones in garlic and oil are nice)
- 125g tuna (one tin)
- Handful of green beans
- 2 hard boiled eggs, each sliced into 6 pieces
- 6 baby new potatoes, cooked and halved/quartered
- Olive oil
- Balsamic vinegar

Directions (15-20 minutes)

Boil the eggs and potatoes. Wash the lettuce and combine the olives, anchovies, green beans and tuna in a salad bowl. When the eggs and potatoes are ready, run them under cold water to cool down. Cut the eggs into quarters and the potatoes in half and add to the salad.

To dress use two parts olive oil to one part balsamic vinegar.

Prawn and Avocado Pasta Salad

Ingredients (serves 2)

- 200g GF pasta
- 20 cooked tiger prawns (defrosted)
- 1 avocado
- 1 spring onion
- 10 cherry tomatoes, halved
- ½ lemon
- Crushed garlic clove
- Olive oil

Directions (15 minutes)

Cook pasta, then drain and rinse under cold water. In a separate bowl add zest and juice of half a lemon, one crushed garlic clove, halved tomatoes and chopped spring onions. Add prawns and slices of avocado last, gently toss, mixing into the pasta. Serve with a drizzle of olive oil and cracked black pepper.

Tip

If storing this pasta to eat later keep the avocado separate until eating.

Tuna Pasta Salad

Ingredients (serves 2)

- 1 tin tuna
- 200g GF pasta
- Handful of sweetcorn
- Small chopped red pepper
- 1 celery stick, chopped
- 2 tbsp mayonnaise

Directions (15 minutes)

Cook the pasta, then drain and rinse under cold water, add a little olive oil to the pasta to stop it sticking. Dice the red pepper and celery then add the sweetcorn, tuna, and mix in the mayonnaise to taste. Squeeze a bit of lemon juice and cracked black pepper on the top.

Green Salad

Green salads can be boring if they just consist of the same old ingredients: lettuce, tomatoes and peppers. To make salads more interesting, try to add in as big a variety as possible and serve vegetables in separate piles on a big bed of lettuce. Try adding protein like cooked chicken, turkey, ham or tuna or add the following vegetables or fruit:

- Spinach and rocket (calcium and iron)
- Grated carrot (vitamin A)
- Sliced beetroot (antioxidants)
- Olives (omega 9)
- Anchovies (omega 3)
- Peppers (full of antioxidants)
- Mushrooms (high in potassium)
- Cauliflower (great source of vitamin C)
- Avocado (omega 9)
- Celery (vitamin C and vitamin K)
- Sweetcorn (vitamin B and vitamin C)
- Radishes (vitamin C plus calcium)
- Asparagus tips (vitamin B and antioxidants)
- Dried apricots (high in calcium)
- Blueberries (high in phytonutrients)
- Grapes (high in vitamin B and vitamin K)

No salad is complete without dressing. Try some of the dressings that follow.

SALAD DRESSINGS

Homemade dressings are quick and easy, taking less than 5 minutes to prepare.

Garlic and mustard dressing

- 6 tbsp olive oil
- 2 tbsp lemon juice
- 1 tbsp Dijon mustard
- ½ clove crushed garlic

Olive oil and tamari dressing

This is quick and easy and is lovely not only on salads but also on steamed vegetables. Tamari is a gluten-free soy sauce.

- 2 tbsp. olive oil
- 1 tbsp tamari

Honey and mustard dressing

- ¼ cup mayonnaise
- 1 tbsp Dijon mustard
- 1 tbsp honey
- ½ tbsp lemon juice

Balsamic vinegar and oil dressing

- 6 tbsp olive oil
- 2 tbsp balsamic vinegar
- Pinch salt and ground black pepper

- ½ tsp sugar
- ¼ clove crushed garlic

Directions

Put the balsamic vinegar and crushed garlic in a bowl with the sugar and whisk until the sugar dissolves. Slowly add the oil and keep whisking. Add a pinch of salt and ground black pepper to taste.

PASTA

Pesto Pasta

This really is a quick and easy one.

Ingredients (serves 2)
- 200g GF Pasta
- Jar Red Pesto
- 2 small chicken breasts

Optional
- Fresh basil

Directions (10 minutes)

Boil pasta and fry diced chunks of chicken breast in a small amount of oil. Drain pasta, add to the frying pan with red pesto sauce and chicken and stir through. Garnish with fresh basil.

Creamy Avocado Pasta

Ingredients (serves 1)

- 1 portion rice noodles
- Juice ½ lemon
- 1 garlic clove
- 1 tbsp olive oil
- ½ avocado
- 1 tbsp basil

Directions (10 minutes)

Cook rice noodles (takes around 8 minutes in a bowl of hot water). In the meantime, combine the lemon, crushed garlic, olive oil, avocado and basil in a blender. When pasta is cooked, drain and stir the sauce through (it makes quite a thick sauce).

Creamy Ham and Vegetable Pasta

This one works well for those who love a creamy sauce but don't want dairy. You can add or take away different ingredients (e.g. if you don't like the spinach or if you want to replace the ham with chicken).

Ingredients (serves 4)

- 1 onion
- 200g ham
- 500ml DF milk (oat milk works well)
- 4tbsp cornflour
- 100g peas
- 100g sweetcorn
- 100g mushrooms
- Spinach (small amount)
- 350g GF pasta

Directions (15 minutes)

Put pasta on to boil. Dice onion and mushroom and brown in a frying pan with a small amount of oil. Make cornflour into a paste by adding approx. 4 tbsp water to the cornflour, then add this to the frying pan. Pour the milk into the frying pan gradually, stirring continuously and keep on a medium to high heat to make the creamy sauce. When the mixture has thickened, add in the ham and vegetables to heat through. Once the pasta has cooked, drain and add to frying pan, stirring the sauce through.

Prawn and Chorizo Pasta

Ingredients (serves 2)

- 20 tiger prawns
- ½ chorizo sausage, cut into chunks
- 'Seeds of Change' organic tomato sauce (or make your own sauce with ½ tin of passata, tin of organic tomatoes, 1 tsp brown sugar and a handful of fresh basil)
- 200g GF Pasta
- 1 small onion
- 1-2 cloves of garlic

Optional
- Spinach

Directions (15 minutes)

Put the pasta on to boil. Fry half an onion and one or two cloves of crushed garlic (if using) in a frying pan with a little oil. Add the tiger prawns until thoroughly cooked through and add thick slices of chorizo sausage to the pan (along with a little chopped spinach for that extra calcium if desired). Add the tomato sauce and when the pasta is cooked add it to the frying pan with the sauce and stir through.

Lemon and Chilli Prawn Pasta

Ingredients (serves 2)

- 20 prawns
- 200g GF pasta
- 4 cloves of garlic
- 100g cherry tomatoes (quartered)
- 2 red chillis (chopped and de-seeded)
- 1 tsp lemon zest
- Juice of half a lemon
- 2 tbsp olive oil
- Fresh basil

Directions (15 minutes)

Put pasta on to boil. Cook prawns in a little oil and add crushed garlic (don't let it burn) and chillis. Add quartered tomatoes, lemon zest and lemon juice and cook for around 2 minutes. Drain the pasta and toss sauce through. Garnish with fresh basil and salt and pepper.

Chicken and Asparagus Pasta

Ingredients (serves 2)

- 200g GF pasta
- 2 chicken breast fillets, cut into strips
- 100g asparagus, cut into small pieces
- 1-2 crushed garlic cloves
- 1 tsp dried chilli flakes

Directions (15 minutes)

Put the pasta on to boil. Fry the chicken in a pan with oil for 6-7 minutes then when nearly finished, add asparagus, garlic cloves and chilli flakes and cook for another two minutes.

Toss in pasta and serve, seasoning with salt and pepper to taste.

STIR FRY

Due to high temperature methods involved in stir-fry recipes I always recommend coconut oil for cooking. If you aren't using coconut oil, use olive oil instead but for health reasons do try and keep away from vegetable oils.

Quick Stir Fry

This is a great staple for a quick meal; the combination of vegetables can be changed according to taste as can the meat.

Ingredients (serves 2)
- 20 tiger prawns (or try chicken or marinated tofu)
- Selection of vegetables (including broccoli, peppers, sugar snap peas, cauliflower, baby corn, courgettes, beansprouts etc. You can also buy stir-fry vegetable packs to make things easy)
- 250g brown rice
- GF stock cube
- Cornflour to thicken
- Fish sauce
- Tamari sauce (wheat-free soy sauce)

Directions (15 minutes)
Fry the chicken in a frying pan with some coconut oil. Add in half a stock cube with 250ml filtered water and thicken with cornflour. Add in the vegetables. Let it bubble. Add fish sauce to taste.

Serve with rice and tamari sauce (to taste).

Tip

Instead of fish and tamari sauce you can use any number of store-bought sauces; check the ingredients carefully and look for organic brands. For example, sweet and sour sauce with chicken, sweetcorn, carrots and peppers.

Tofu and Greens with Cashew Nuts

Tofu, soya beans, broccoli and pak choi all contain high levels of calcium; this is a great recipe to increase your calcium levels when you are dairy free.

Ingredients (serves 2)
- 200g marinated tofu pieces
- ½ head of broccoli
- 1 head pak choi
- 100g soya beans
- 25g cashew nuts
- 2 diced spring onions
- 2 cloves garlic
- 2 tbsp hoisin sauce
- 1 tbsp tamari sauce
- ½ red chilli, deseeded and finely chopped

Directions (15 minutes)

Heat a teaspoon of coconut oil in a frying pan. Add the broccoli and fry on a high heat for around 5 minutes until tender. Add the garlic and chilli then toss through the spring onions, soya beans (if these are from frozen you can add them to the pan just after the broccoli), pak choi and tofu. Add the nut, hoisin sauce and tamari sauce just at the end to warm through.

Egg Fried Rice

Ingredients (serves 2)

- 20 tiger prawns
- ½ onion
- Small clove of garlic
- Handful of peas
- Handful of sweetcorn
- 250g brown rice (2 min microwave pack is fine)
- 1 egg
- Thai sweet chilli sauce

Directions (15 minutes)

Fry the onion in a frying pan with a small amount of oil. While the onion is cooking, put a 2 minute pack of basmati rice in the microwave. Add crushed garlic and tiger prawns to the frying pan, add frozen peas directly to pan as well. When the rice is ready, add the rice and sweetcorn to the pan with a little more oil and stir together. Crack an egg into the frying pan and mix through at the end.

Serve with Thai sweet chilli sauce or tamari sauce.

Chicken and Rice

This one is really quick and very tasty – I make this whenever I'm tempted to get a Chinese food take-out – it is even quicker than waiting in the local takeaway and much tastier!

So, instead of stopping at your local takeaway on a Friday night, stop at your local supermarket deli counter instead and pick up one of their cooked chickens. Directions as follows:

Ingredients (serves 2)
- Pre-cooked chicken pieces
- 2 spring onions, chopped
- 100g broccoli
- 250g brown rice
- Tamari sauce (wheat-free soy sauce)

Directions (15 minutes)
Put the rice in the microwave for 2 minutes and start steaming the broccoli. Fry the chopped spring onions in a pan with a little bit of oil. Shred the chicken into pieces, add the rice and broccoli to the pan and serve with tamari sauce.

Thai Green Curry

This recipe was given to me by my friend Sarah. You can make the sauce from scratch as below or for the really quick version you can also just buy the curry paste and add coconut milk (one brand is Thai Taste Gang Keow Wan).

Ingredients (serves 6-8)
- 2 stalks of lemongrass
- 4-6 green chillis (chopped and deseeded)
- 2 large garlic cloves
- 2 spring onions, roughly chopped
- 2 limes grated zest and juice
- 5cm piece ginger (grated)
- Large bunch of fresh coriander chopped
- 2 tsp cumin
- 2 tsp of tamari sauce
- 800g chicken (or prawns)
- 2 tins Coconut milk
- Rice noodles (or rice)

Directions (20 minutes)
Blitz the above spices in the blender and fry in oil with prawns or chicken. Add coconut milk and serve with rice noodles or rice. If the coconut sauce is too rich you can add in chicken stock.

Optional
Sarah also recommends adding in red peppers or bamboo shoots.

Paella

This is a recipe that my friend Hannah has given me. When cooking from scratch it takes around 40 minutes but if you batch cook and freeze the sauce it only take 15 minutes to heat up as a risotto afterwards. It is fantastic; easy to freeze and quick to prepare after defrost; this is a firm family favourite in our house.

Ingredients (serves 8)
- 6 chicken thighs
- 1 large onion
- 2 or 3 cloves of garlic
- 1 red pepper
- 400g tin of tomatoes
- 400g tin of passata
- Pinch of saffron
- Teaspoon of paprika
- 2 flat tablespoons of oregano
- GF chicken stock cube
- Fish stock cube
- 400g frozen bag of seafood
- 150g frozen peas

Directions (40 minutes)

For chicken tomato sauce:
Fry the chicken thighs in oil to seal. Remove from pan then fry a large onion and two or three cloves of garlic. Add the chicken back in and then add the chopped pepper plus one tin of tomatoes and a tin of passata.

CO GLUTEN AND DAIRY FREE AND FEEL GREAT!

To season add a pinch of saffron, a teaspoon of paprika and two flat tablespoons of oregano. Let it bubble. Take half the mixture and add a chicken stock cube and the other half and add a fish stock cube. Freeze.

To make risotto:
Defrost your chicken tomato sauce in the microwave and as it is defrosting, start cooking risotto rice. Put oil in a pan and start adding boiled water to risotto rice, let it cook. As soon as the mixture is defrosted pour all of it into the pan so there is a lot of tomato juice.

To make the paella even more interesting, follow the instructions above and when the rice has nearly finished cooking, add a frozen bag of seafood (king prawns, calamari etc.) so the latent heat cooks them through. Add the frozen peas last. It takes around 15 minutes to make this from defrost.

CHICKEN

Chicken Kebabs with Apricot Jam

Ingredients (serves 2)

- 2 organic chicken breasts
- Apricot jam
- Choice of vegetables including onions, red peppers, mushrooms, courgettes etc.

Directions (15 minutes)

Cut chicken into chunks and thread onto skewers along with chosen vegetables. Grill in the oven. When halfway through cooking, take out and brush with jam. Put back in oven to finish.

Serve with on a bed of rice or with mashed potatoes.

Optional

Instead of apricot jam, you can also use either mango chutney, sweet Thai chilli sauce or apple sauce

Cheat's Roast Chicken Dinner

Ingredients (serves 2)

- 2 organic chicken breasts
- 4 carrots
- ½ head broccoli
- 2 potatoes

Optional
- Garlic
- Lemon

Directions (20 minutes)

Put potatoes in microwave oven for 8-10 minutes. Cut the chicken breast into strips, place on a baking tray and drizzle with olive oil. (Add seasonings if you wish – e.g. crushed garlic or lemon juice). When the potatoes are finished, add them to the oven with the chicken to finish them off so they get a crispy baked coating.

Steam the carrots and broccoli. Serve all with 'cheats' store-bought gluten-free gravy and Yorkshire puddings. (Note: there is a recipe for homemade gluten and dairy-free gravy and Yorkshire puddings in the 'Sunday Gourmet' section).

Homemade Chicken Nuggets and Potato Wedges

After the horror pictures circulating on social media of the pink 'goo' which makes up most varieties of commercialised chicken nuggets, I took to making my own, following a recipe that I had seen my friend Caroline do for her children. This probably takes a little longer to make at 15-20 minutes but it is well worth it!

Ingredients (serves 2-3)
- 2 organic chicken breasts
- GF breadcrumbs (with a pinch of salt and pepper)
- 1 Egg
- 4 carrots
- 2 corn on the cob
- 2 potatoes

Optional
- Rosemary
- Ketchup

Directions (20 minutes)
Heat a small amount of oil on a baking tray (coconut oil works really well here) in the oven at a high temperature – around 220 degrees. Cut the potatoes into wedges and place them on the baking tray (when the oil is hot enough the potatoes will sizzle when added). Sprinkle some rosemary on top and put back in the oven, turning the temperature down to around 200 degrees.

Cut the chicken into cubes, dip in whisked egg and roll in breadcrumbs. Place on a baking tray and put into the oven as well, turning the temperature down to about 180 degrees. Cook for around 15 minutes or until the breadcrumbs are golden and the wedges are cooked through.

Steam the carrots and corn (around 5 minutes). Serve with ketchup!

Chicken with Roasted Tomatoes and Asparagus

Ingredients (serves 4)

- 4 organic chicken breasts, cut into strips
- 30 sweet baby tomatoes
- 4 tbsp Thai sweet chilli sauce
- 350g brown rice
- 200g asparagus

Directions (20 minutes)

Cut the chicken breast into strips and place in a roasting dish with the washed baby tomatoes. Drizzle chicken in olive oil and a tbsp of Thai sweet chilli sauce for each breast. Cover with foil and cook in the oven at 180 degrees for about 20 minutes. Steam the asparagus for 5 minutes and cook the brown rice (the 2 minute microwave brown rice packs are easy).

Chicken with Mango Sauce

Ingredients (serves 4)

- 4 organic chicken breasts
- 2 tbsp mango chutney
- 3 tbsp cornflour, made into a paste with 3 tbsp water
- 400ml rice milk

Directions (30 minutes)

Cut the chicken breasts in half and seal in a frying pan with a little oil (coconut oil adds a lovely flavour here). Add the cornflour paste to a saucepan with the rice milk and heat until the sauce becomes thick (you can add more cornflour for a thicker sauce depending on your preference). Add in 2 tbsp mango chutney to taste (more mango makes it sweeter rather than creamier). Put the chicken in an oven dish and cover with the sauce. Cook in the oven at 180 degrees for 20-25 minutes.

LAMB

Lamb Kebabs

Ingredients (serves 3-4)

- 400g minced lamb
- 1 red onion, finely diced
- 1-2 cloves garlic
- Handful of mixed herbs

Optional

- Lemon zest
- Cube of frozen spinach
- GF breadcrumbs
- Egg

Directions (20 minutes)

Combine lamb, finely diced onion, crushed garlic, lemon zest, defrosted spinach and mixed herbs in a bowl. Add gluten-free breadcrumbs for texture and egg to help the mixture stick together (note if you are allergic to egg you do not have to add it; the kebabs won't stick together as well but they will taste just as good!). Form the meat around skewers and place on a baking tray. Put in the oven for 10-12 minutes or until cooked through.

Serve with cucumber dipping yoghurt or salsa plus salad and rice.

Cucumber Yoghurt Dipping Sauce

Ingredients

- 250ml natural soya yoghurt
- ½ grated or finely chopped cucumber
- Large handful mint leaves, chopped
- Pinch salt

Directions (5 minutes)

Grate or chop the cucumber and wrap in a tea towel to squeeze out the excess liquid. Combine all of the ingredients together and serve.

Lamb Chops with Mint Sauce, New Potatoes and Peas

Ingredients (serves 4)

- 400g organic free-range lamb chops
- 80g mint sauce
- 500g new potatoes
- 300g peas

Directions (20 minutes)

Grill the lamb chops at 220 degrees C for around 15-20 minutes. Boil the new potatoes for around 10-15 minutes or until cooked and steam the peas for 2 minutes. Serve with mint sauce.

Homemade Mint Sauce

Ingredients

- 20g chopped mint
- Pinch of salt
- 1 tbsp caster sugar
- 4 tbsp white wine vinegar

Directions (5 minutes)

My grandma used to grow mint in her garden and making your own mint sauce is very easy: simply take a bunch of chopped mint, a pinch of salt and 1 tbsp of caster sugar. Add 4 tbsp of boiling water and 4 tbsp of white wine vinegar to taste.

Shepherd's Pie with Sweet Potato Mash

Shepherd's Pie was a favourite when I was a child (my mum used to tell us that my dad had been to collect the shepherds that morning!). It's great winter comfort food and freezes well. This is my version of my mum's recipe.

Ingredients (serves 4)

- 400g organic minced lamb
- 1 onion
- 2 cloves garlic
- 2 carrots
- 600g sweet potatoes
- Handful of broccoli
- Handful of peas
- Handful of sweetcorn
- Small cube frozen spinach
- Mixed herbs

For the gravy

- GF lamb stock cube
- Gravy browning
- Cornflour
- Low sugar HP sauce (optional – note HP sauce contains rye and barley so those strictly gluten free rather than wheat free must not use this)

Directions (40 minutes)

Fry the onions then garlic, add in the mince, a sprinkling of mixed herbs, and brown. In a separate pot, steam the carrots, broccoli, peas and sweetcorn. Defrost the spinach in the microwave for two minutes, and when this is finished put the sweet potatoes in the microwave to bake.

Drain the frying pan of the meat juices and collect in a clear container. Let the fat settle to the top and skim this off. Use the juices of the meat to make gravy using cornflour with water to thicken, plus the water that the vegetables were cooked in with a GF stock cube added. To add colour to the gravy use gravy browning. Season to taste.

Combine the mince mixture, vegetables and gravy and transfer to freezable containers. Top with mashed sweet potato. Sweet potato mash can be made using dairy-free butter, milk, and salt and pepper to season.

Optional:
- Adding spinach and broccoli is optional (possibly best not tried with junior fussy eaters)
- If sweet potato mash is too orange, then you can also try mashing a bit of swede with white potatoes and see if that goes unnoticed instead
- The key is to add a small amount of vegetables – not so many that they put everyone off eating the dish!
- Mushrooms and courgettes can also be added to Shepherd's Pie and make a great substitute for other veg if they are not liked
- You can serve this with lacto fermented vegetables like picked cabbage or sauerkraut for an added zing

PORK

Pork Medallions with Apple Sauce and Sweet Potato Mash
Ingredients (serves 4)

- 400g pork medallions (or pork chops)
- 80g apple sauce
- 300g green beans
- 600g sweet potatoes

Directions (10-15 minutes)
Put the potatoes in the microwave for 6-8 minutes. Grill or fry the pork chops and steam the green beans. Once cooked, peel and mash the sweet potatoes with dairy-free spread. Serve with apple sauce.

Homemade Apple Sauce
Ingredients

- 4 apples
- 150ml water
- 50g sugar
- Tsp cinnamon

Directions (20-25 minutes)
Peel, core and chop the apples. Put in a pan with 150ml of water and 50g of sugar plus a tsp of cinnamon. Heat together in a pan until the apples are soft, and mash.

Sausages, Beans and Mash

This meal is a firm favourite with the picky eaters in my house, but it doesn't have to be an unhealthy choice, as long as you are particular about what you buy.

Ingredients (serves 4)

- 400g sausages – look for gluten-free, organic, full-pork products free from sulphites or other preservatives
- 250g beans – (tinned beans are ok – try to get the reduced salt and sugar variety)
- 500g potatoes (again, choose organic if you can or sweet potatoes)

Directions (20 minutes)

Grill the sausages for 15-20 minutes rather than frying, and boil the potatoes. Mash the potatoes with a dairy-free butter, and you could also add in dairy-free cheese or crushed garlic. Or, instead of mash, jacket potatoes with their skins on is a healthier choice. Heat beans in a pan and serve.

Pork Chop Hotpot

Pork can be tough so using a slow cooker is a great way to tenderise the meat.

Ingredients (serves 4)
- 4 organic pork chops
- 16-20 shallots
- 2 garlic cloves, peeled and crushed
- 50g sun dried tomatoes
- 400g organic chopped tomatoes
- 150ml red wine
- 150ml GF chicken stock
- 2 tbsp oregano

Directions (10 minutes prep, 5 hours cooking)
Fry the pork chops in a little oil with the shallots and garlic for 5 minutes. Remove from the frying pan and add to slow cooker with the tomatoes, red wine, chicken stock and herbs. Cook on a low heat for 5 hours and serve with green beans and new potatoes.

BEEF

Homemade Burgers or Meatballs

Ingredients (serves 4)

- 400g minced organic beef
- 4 tbsp tomato paste
- 50g spinach
- 1 onion, diced
- 2-3 cloves crushed garlic
- 1.5 tbsp parsley
- 1 egg
- 75g GF breadcrumbs

Directions (20 minutes)

Combine all the ingredients together in a bowl and mix together with hands. Form burgers from mixture and grill. You can also wrap burgers individually in greaseproof paper to freeze and use later. Serve with salad and jacket potatoes.

The same mixture can also be used to make meatballs which you can defrost and add to bolognaise sauce to serve with GF pasta.

Tacos with Guacamole and Salsa

The following is a homemade taco recipe but to save time you can also buy taco packs plus salsa and guacamole from the supermarket which are quick and easy – but not quite as tasty! Note to be careful to check any store-bought guacamole for added dairy products like cream.

Ingredients (serves 4)
- 400g organic minced beef
- 8 taco corn shells
- 1 tablespoon chilli powder
- ¼ teaspoon garlic powder
- ¼ teaspoon onion powder
- ¼ teaspoon red pepper flakes
- ¼ teaspoon dried oregano
- ½ teaspoon paprika
- 1.5 teaspoons cumin
- 1 teaspoon salt
- 1 teaspoon black pepper

Directions (25 minutes)
Fry the minced beef. Combine seasoning in a bowl and sprinkle over the meat with ⅓ cup of water. Let it bubble and infuse. Warm the taco shells in the oven for 2 minutes. Serve meat in taco shells with little gem lettuce, salsa and guacamole.

Salsa
Ingredients

- 4 tomatoes
- 1 green chilli

- 1 red pepper
- Lime zest and juice of one lime
- 2 tbsp parsley

Directions (5 minutes)

Chop the ingredients and mix together in a small bowl.

Guacamole

Ingredients

- 2 large avocados
- Juice of 1 lemon
- 3 cloves garlic, crushed
- 2 tbsp olive oil
- 1 spring onion, finely chopped
- Salt and black pepper

Directions (5-10 minutes)

Mash or blend all ingredients except the onion. Stir in chopped onion at the end.

Spaghetti Bolognaise

My friend Nikki is a naturopath and this is her recipe. She recommends adding 50-100ml of bone broth to all stews, soups and gravies whenever possible. Bone broth is rich in many nutrients and amino acids and is used widely by naturopaths to heal the gut and digestive tract. Her amazing spag bol recipe is below, and more information on making bone broth can be found in the 'soups' section.

Ingredients (serves 4)

- 400g organic minced beef
- 1 onion
- 1 celery stalk
- 125g mushrooms
- 1 red pepper
- 1 carrot
- Bay leaf
- Bolognaise sauce (you can use an organic store-bought one or make your own using ½ tin of passata, one tin of chopped organic tomatoes and a tbsp of basil. Add a little brown sugar if you wish)

Optional

- Cube of frozen spinach
- 50ml bone broth (from freezer – see 'soups' section)

Directions (40 minutes)

Fry onion in coconut oil. Finely chop celery, mushrooms and red pepper and add to the frying pan so they go really soft. Add bay leaf. Put mince into pan to brown, then grate a carrot and add to the mix. Add tomato sauce and serve with GF pasta.

Chilli Con Carne

Ingredients (serves 4)

- 400g organic beef mince
- 1 chopped onion
- 1 chopped red pepper
- 6-8 chopped mushrooms
- 3 cloves garlic
- 1 tsp hot chilli powder
- 1 tsp paprika
- 1tsp ground cumin
- ½ tsp marjoram
- 2 tbsp dried mixed herbs
- 250g kidney beans
- 250g chick peas
- 400g tinned chopped organic tomatoes
- 400g passata
- 1 beef GF stock cube

Directions (40 minutes)

Brown the chopped onions, mushrooms, and peppers in oil and add the mince plus crushed garlic. Once the mince has browned, sprinkle the chilli powder, paprika, cumin, marjoram and mixed herbs into the pan along with the kidney beans and chick peas. Add in the chopped tomatoes, passata, and crumble in a beef stock cube (you can add some water to the stock cube – or a bit of bone broth – depending how thick you want your sauce.)

Serve with brown rice.

Grandma Goulden's Hotpot Stew

This is my grandma's hotpot recipe which was a firm favourite of mine as a child.

Ingredients (serves 4)

- 400g organic braising or stewing steak
- 3 carrots
- ¼ swede (half the portion of the carrots)
- ½ leek
- 3 large potatoes
- Cornflour to thicken
- Gluten-free stock cubes
- Gravy browning

Directions (1.5 hours)

Cut the meat into approximately 1 inch cubes and put in a pan. Peel and thickly slice several carrots and the swede. Cut the swede into the same sized chunks as the carrots and use half the amount of swede to carrots. Add to the pan with the meat and add enough cold filtered water to cover. Put the pan on the hob and bring to the boil. Turn down the heat and simmer until the meat is tender (you can tell when it's tender by eating a piece!). This will probably take at least an hour.

When the meat is cooked, add half a peeled and chopped leek, plus the peeled and sliced potatoes, to the pan.

To thicken and add flavour to the mixture, crumble 1-2 gluten-free stock cubes into the pan (I find you may need to use more than one stock cube when they are gluten-free). You can also thicken the mixture a little at this point with cornflour (add a dash of water to a tablespoon of cornflour in a separate container to mix together first), and add a drop of gravy browning for colour if you wish.

Simmer the mixture until the potatoes are soft but still formed (around 20 minutes).

Serve with fresh beetroot or pickled vegetables such as sauerkraut.

Beef and Ale Stew

Ingredients (serves 4)

- 2 celery stalks
- 2 carrots
- 1 onion
- 50g spinach
- 400g diced organic beef
- 1 tin of chopped tomatoes
- 500ml Guinness
- 2 bay leaves
- GF stock cube
- HP Sauce (optional – not gluten free)
- 1 tbsp GF flour

Directions (10 minutes prep, 3-4 hours cooking)
Put the chopped celery, carrots and onion in a slow cooker with a little oil. Add the beef, 1 tablespoon of GF flour, the chopped tomatoes, Guinness, dried bay leaves and chopped spinach. Crumble in a stock cube and a dash of HP sauce to taste (not essential). Leave in the pot on a low heat for 3-4 hours.

Tip
You can do this same recipe substituting chicken and white wine or lamb and red wine.

FISH

Fish is not only healthy but it is quick and easy to prepare. I typically bake fish wrapped in aluminium foil in the oven but add something to the top of it to make it a bit more interesting. For instance:

- Green pesto
- Wholegrain mustard
- Sweet Thai chilli sauce
- Lemon zest, dairy-free spread with ground black pepper and chillis
- Thousand Island dressing with chopped olives
- GF breadcrumbs for a crunch

Seasoned Seabass Steaks with Quinoa, Baby Corn and Mange Touts

Ingredients (serves 2)

- 2 seabass fillets
- 1 tsbp dairy-free spread
- 1/2 tsp sage
- 1/2 tsp chives
- 1/2 tsp lemon zest
- 250g quinoa
- Baby corn
- Mange touts

Directions (15 minutes)

Combine dairy-free butter, sage, chives and lemon rind in bowl and mix. Season seabass with mixture, add salt and pepper if desired, wrap in tin foil and bake in the oven at 180 degrees for 10-12 minutes.

Serve with steamed baby corn, mange touts and quinoa.

Honey Soy Salmon with Salad

Ingredients (serves 2)

- 2 salmon fillets
- 1 tbsp honey
- 1 tbsp tamari sauce (gluten-free soy sauce)
- Salad: lettuce, peppers, grated carrot, spring onions, olives etc.

Directions (15 minutes)

Season salmon fillet with sea salt and pepper. Combine 1 tablespoon of honey with 1 teaspoon of tamari sauce and drizzle over the salmon. Wrap salmon in tin foil and bake in the oven for 10-15 minutes. Serve warm with side salad.

Tuna Steaks with Tomatoes, Olives and Rice

This was my husband's main bachelor meal. The tuna steaks were always from frozen but this is actually a better nutritional choice than tinned tuna, which doesn't contain the same amount of omega 3 as the full steaks do.

Ingredients (serves 2)
- 2 tuna steaks
- 250g chopped organic tomatoes
- 10 black olives, chopped
- 250g brown rice

Optional
- Onion
- Garlic
- Capers

Directions (20 minutes)

Fry the tuna steaks in a frying pan in a little oil with a small amount of diced onion and a crushed garlic bulb (if using). Add a tin of chopped organic tomatoes and some chopped black olives. Add capers for an extra zing if desired.

Serve with rice and season with cracked black pepper.

Homemade Fish Fingers Served with Broccoli and Sweet Potato Mash

Ingredients (serves 2)

- 2 cod steaks, cut into strips
- ½ tsp balsamic vinegar
- ⅛ tsp salt
- ⅛ tsp paprika
- 1 egg
- 120g GF breadcrumbs
- Broccoli
- Sweet potato wedges

Directions (20 minutes)

Preheat oven to 200 degrees. Mix balsamic vinegar, salt, paprika and breadcrumbs together. Brush the cod fillets with egg and dip into seasoned GF breadcrumb mixture. Bake in the oven for 10 minutes.

Serve with steamed broccoli and sweet potato mash.

Fish Cakes

Ingredients (serves 2)

- 200g fish
- 250g potatoes
- 50g GF breadcrumbs
- 1 tsp parsley
- 1 tsp lemon zest
- GF flour

Directions (20 minutes)

Boil and mash the potatoes. Mix cooked fish, mash and breadcrumbs. Add parsley and lemon zest. Form mixture into flat cakes and fry until golden on each side.

Optional

- You can also add a sprinkling of sesame seeds for extra crunch

Fish Bake

Ingredients (serves 2)

- 200g salmon and cod in chunks (or a fish pie mix from the supermarket)
- 10-12 asparagus spears
- Black pepper
- ½ lemon, juiced and grated for zest
- 2 tbsp olive oil
- 10-12 new potatoes, halved

Directions (25 minutes)

Put the fish and potatoes on a baking tray and drizzle with olive oil; add crushed and grated lemon zest and black pepper. Bake at 200 degrees in the oven for 10 minutes. Add the asparagus and bake for another 10 minutes.

Sushi

Sushi is surprisingly easy to make (and children love to help you with this one too!)

Ingredients
- Tuna fish (or preferred seafood – prawns, crab or salmon)
- Finely sliced cucumber, carrot, pepper, radishes (or preferred vegetable)
- Sushi rice
- Unsalted dried seaweed
- Rice wine vinegar
- Sugar
- Salt

Optional
- Wasabi
- Pickled ginger
- Tamari sauce
- Sesame seeds

Directions (40 minutes)

Cook the sushi rice (follow the instructions on the pack but note that it will need around 30 minutes to soak before cooking). Cut vegetables into strips. Drain the rice once it has cooked and put in a bowl. In a separate bowl mix two tablespoons of rice wine vinegar plus some sugar and salt (to preferred taste) until it dissolves. Add this mixture to the rice and mix thoroughly. You can then roll the rice up into seaweed parcels with your preferred mix of vegetable, seafood and sesame seeds. Garnish with wasabi, tamari sauce and pickled ginger to taste.

Pirate's Pie

My children will only eat fish pie if we call it Pirate's Pie. You can make this when you have time in separate freezable bowls and it keeps and defrosts well.

Ingredients (serves 4)
- 400g salmon
- 2 sliced leeks
- 1 clove of garlic
- 600g mashed potato
- 500ml DF milk
- 2 tbsp cornflour
- 100g peas

Optional
- Lemon zest
- Spinach (frozen cube of diced spinach)

Directions (50 minutes)
Fry leeks and garlic in oil and then add fish. Add cold water to the cornflour to make a paste, then stir in cornflour and milk to make a creamy sauce. Add lemon zest to taste and defrosted frozen peas and spinach. Top with mashed potato and freeze.

Before eating, defrost thoroughly and bake in the oven for 30 minutes at 200 degrees C.

SNACKS

Ideas for quick, healthy, gluten and dairy-free snacks:

- Dried fruit – cranberries, raisins, apricots, mango, pineapple
- Fruit – banana, tangerine, apples, grapes, strawberries, cherries (try coconut yoghurt with your fruit salad – this is really yummy!)
- Sweet potato with dairy-free spread (cook in microwave and mash up – quick and easy to do)
- Rice cakes (plain or with nut butters)
- Carrots, cucumber, cherry tomatoes, celery, hummus
- Soya yoghurt
- Fruit bars (concentrated fruit with no added sugar e.g. HumZingers or School Bars)
- Kiwi fruit cut in half to eat with a spoon
- Nuts and seeds (nuts and seeds are very healthy and contain a number of nutrients including high levels of good fats as well as calcium)
- Peanut butter and gluten-free breadsticks/crackers or peanut butter with celery sticks
- Olives
- Monkey peanuts are great – fun to crack open for kids and tasty
- Crisps – try to have reduced salt, baked crisps or vegetable crisps. Most crisps are gluten and dairy free but any food which is fried in fat at high temperatures is really not good for you

If you have more time:

Artichoke hearts

Sprinkle drained canned artichoke hearts with lemon zest, capers, chopped fresh basil and olive oil. Eat with toothpicks.

Cucumber crackers

Turn cucumber slices into crackers: Spread them with olive tapenade and garnish with chopped fresh tarragon.

Homemade popcorn

Make your own in a pan with coconut oil. Heat a teaspoon of coconut oil in a saucepan at a high temperature, add a handful of popcorn kernels and cover the pan with a lid (ideally a glass or transparent pan lid). Leave the heat on high, shaking the pan intermittently. The popcorn kernels will pop when they are hot enough (after 2-3 minutes normally). Be careful to leave the lid on as you don't want to be hit by a popping kernel! You can drizzle with dairy-free butter and salt.

Crunchy chickpeas

Drain a can of chickpeas and place on a baking tray – add some salt and cayenne pepper and drizzle with olive oil. Bake in the oven at 220 degrees for about 30 minutes, turning halfway.

(Note: I roast the pumpkin seeds out of the children's Halloween pumpkin like this (or after you have made pumpkin soup!)

TREATS

Treats are an important part of sticking to a dairy and gluten-free diet. Just don't overdo them or you could end up still feeling rubbish! Here are some ideas to start:

- Fruit and marshmallow skewers dipped in melted dairy-free chocolate
- Jelly – add fruit to your jelly (like pineapple or oranges) for extra interest (and vitamins!)
- If resorting to store-bought sweets, cakes and biscuits, try to choose certain brands. The 'Natural Confectionary Company' make gummy sweets which obviously contain loads of sugar but not too much nasty other stuff
- There are several brands of dairy-free ice cream or fruit sorbets to try – I like the 'Swedish Glace' one which is made with soya beans and has a creamy vanilla taste
- Hot chocolate: use a cocoa powder (I use Green and Black's organics) with DF milk and half a teaspoon of golden granulated sugar

Other sweet treats include:

Homemade Ice Lollies

Directions (5 minutes)

These are really easy to make – you just need to buy the moulds. You can make them with any combination of fruit smoothie or simply pour fresh, not-from-concentrate juice into the moulds and freeze. You can also experiment with different juices and add honey, blended fresh fruit or soya yoghurt.

Chocolate Crackles

Ingredients (makes 16-20)

- 500g DF chocolate
- 250g cornflakes
- 4 tbsp DF spread

Directions (15 minutes plus cooling time)

Melt the DF spread and chocolate in a pan; stir in cornflakes. When the cornflakes are coated in the chocolate mixture, spoon them out into cupcake cases and refrigerate until cool.

Marshmallow Krispies

Ingredients (makes 20-24)

- 50g DF spread
- 300g mini marshmallows
- 200g Rice Krispies

Directions (15 minutes plus cooling time)

Melt the DF spread in a pan on a low heat then add the marshmallows. When the mixture is melted and gooey, turn off the heat and stir in the Rice Krispies. Spread the mixture into a greased 8-10 inch tin and refrigerate. When cool, cut into squares.

Gingerbread

Ingredients (makes approx. 16)

- 350g GF flour
- 100g DF butter
- 1 egg
- 175g of sugar
- 4 tbsp golden syrup
- 1 tsp bicarbonate of soda
- 1.5 tsp ginger

Directions (25 minutes)

Mix together the DF butter, GF flour, ginger and bicarbonate of soda with your fingers until it is crumbly. Add the sugar, syrup, and egg, and mix with a spoon until it forms a firm dough. Dust the rolling surface with GF flour to prevent sticking and roll the mixture flat. Use cookie cutters to cut into different shapes and bake in the oven at 200 degrees C for 15 minutes.

Chocolate Chip Cookies

Ingredients (makes 20)

- 3 mashed bananas (ripe)
- ⅓ cup apple sauce
- 2 cups oats
- ¼ cup almond milk
- ⅓ cup DF chocolate chips
- 1 tsp vanilla
- 1 tsp cinnamon

Directions (25 minutes)

Mix the ingredients together. Drop chunks onto greaseproof paper and bake at 180 degrees C for 15-20 minutes.

Banana Cake

Ingredients

- 100g DF spread
- 250g granulated brown sugar
- 6 mashed bananas
- 200g GF flour
- 1tsp cinnamon

Directions (30 minutes)

Melt DF spread and sugar together in a pan, take off the heat. Mash up bananas and add to the mix with the flour, sprinkle cinnamon into the mixture. Bake at 180 degrees C for 20-25 minutes or until golden brown.

Flapjacks

Ingredients (makes 30)

- 750g DF spread
- 450g golden syrup
- 500g golden granulated sugar
- 1kg porridge oats

Directions (40 minutes)

Line an 8 inch baking tin with greaseproof baking paper. Melt the DF spread in a pan and add the golden syrup and sugar to the butter and heat gently. Once the sugar is dissolved, stir in the porridge oats and mix well. Pack the mixture into the baking tray and cook at 150 degrees for about 30-40 minutes.

Optional

You can add a few tablespoons of mixed seeds (e.g. sesame, sunflower, flax or pumpkin seeds) or also try dried fruit (raisins, cherries or cranberries).

Chocolate Brownies

Ingredients (16 brownies)

- 150g organic DF chocolate
- 100g coconut oil
- 100g golden granulated sugar
- 200g DF flour
- ½ tsp baking powder
- 2 organic free-range eggs
- ½ tsp salt
- 1 tbsp vanilla (also try ½ tsp vanilla and ½ teaspoon of mint for a minty flavour)
- DF chocolate chips

Directions (45 minutes)

Melt the chocolate and coconut oil in a saucepan over a low heat. In a mixing bowl, combine the flour, sugar, salt, and baking powder, and then add two beaten eggs, vanilla extract, and melted dark chocolate and oil mixture. Beat for two minutes until it becomes thick.

Add mixture to a greased baking tin and cook at 180 degrees C for 35 minutes.

Lemon Drizzle Cake

Ingredients

- 200g DF spread
- 200g caster sugar
- 2 eggs
- 200g GF flour
- Zest from two lemons
- 4 tbsp lemon juice
- 1 tbsp poppy seeds
- 2 tbsp icing sugar

Directions (60 minutes)

Beat the DF spread and sugar together with an electric mixer until the mixture is light and fluffy. Lightly beat the eggs in a separate bowl with a tablespoon of flour, and add in the lemon zest, poppy seeds, 2 tbsp lemon juice and rest of the flour. Combine both mixtures then put in a greased cake tin. Bake in the oven for 45 minutes at 180 degrees C.

Once the cake has cooled, drizzle with icing made from the icing sugar and 2 tbsp of lemon juice.

THE SUNDAY GOURMET

I n our house, Sunday is family time and about the only day of the week we get to catch up. I try to ensure that this is my day to get organised for the week ahead and any baking or more time consuming cooking I do tends to be on this day. Of course, every household is different and the following recipes are for those occasions when you can indulge yourself, and have a little more time to spare.

Sunday Breakfast/Brunch
Instead of the weekly 'grab and go' it is nice at least one day a week to have a leisurely start and time to make something tasty to eat. Try the following recipes to mix up your weekly routine.

Vegetable Frittata

Ingredients (serves 1)

- 4 organic free-range eggs
- ½ chopped onion
- ½ chopped pepper
- 6 chopped mushrooms
- Handful of chopped spinach

Directions (15 minutes)

Beat the eggs until they are light and frothy. Put some oil in a non-stick frying pan and place on a medium heat. Pour the egg mixture into the pan and allow eggs to start cooking. Scatter the vegetables over the top of the eggs and when they are mainly set, fold the frittata in half and slide onto a plate. (I like this one served with ketchup!)

American Style Blueberry Pancakes

American pancakes differ from those in the UK as there is sugar added to the batter; it is also a much thicker batter producing fatter, fluffier pancakes.

Ingredients (serves 4)

- 200g GF flour
- 100g golden granulated sugar
- 2 eggs
- Pinch salt
- 100 ml rice milk
- Handful of blueberries
- Maple syrup

Directions (15 minutes)

Whisk the flour, sugar, eggs, and milk in a bowl (you may want to use slightly less milk depending on how big your eggs are and how runny the batter is – the consistency should be like custard). Fold the blueberries into the batter. Put some oil in a frying pan and spoon the batter out about 1.5 tablespoons at a time. Serve with honey or maple syrup. Delicious!

Canadian French Toast

I grew up in Canada and what we call 'Eggy Bread' in the UK was known as French toast in Canada. It was a weekend treat for us.

Ingredients (serves 4-6)

- GF bread (plain white bread works best for this recipe – the seeded bread doesn't taste quite right!)
- 6 eggs
- 30ml DF milk
- Pinch of salt
- Icing sugar

Directions (20 minutes)

Whisk the eggs in a bowl and add a small amount of milk and a pinch of salt. Put the mixture in a shallow dish and soak the bread on both sides in the egg. Place in a frying pan with a bit of oil and fry on both sides. Serve warm and sprinkled with icing sugar on top.

English Breakfast

Directions (20 minutes)

Grilled organic bacon and gluten-free sausages, free-range poached eggs (a really simple way to make poached eggs is in a bowl of boiling water in the microwave. For slightly runny eggs, crack two medium sized eggs into approx. 250ml of boiling water and heat on high in the microwave for 2 minutes), garlic mushrooms and tomatoes (fry chopped mushrooms and tomatoes in coconut oil with a clove of crushed garlic and a pinch of chilli to taste. Garnish with chopped parsley.)

You can serve this with GF bread but I have found that I don't need the bread to fill me up after all that!

Roast Dinners

Roast dinners can be time consuming, but once you have the hang of them, you can get everything ready in around 1.5 hours, depending on the quantity of meat.

I tend to use roasting bags for most meats as it seals in the juices and flavour. I buy an organic joint and will vary whether we have chicken, lamb or beef. A nice marinade with chicken is honey and lemon or simply dairy-free butter seasoned with salt and pepper. My favourite way to marinade lamb is with rosemary, garlic, olive oil and lemon zest. Beef can be tough if you are not careful and a garlic and red wine marinade works well here.

In terms of accompaniments to serve with a roast dinner, some ideas are below:

Gravy

My mother-in-law taught me how to make gravy and it is quite a technique!

Ingredients
- Drained juices from roasted meat
- 3 tbsp cornflour
- GF stock cube
- 500ml filtered water
- Few drops gravy browning

Directions (10 minutes)

Drain the juices from the roasting dish that contains your roast dinner into a clear glass jug. Let the liquid rest until the fat separates to the top of the jug and skim this off with a spoon.

Put 2-3 tablespoons of cornflour in a separate container and add a dash of cold water – just enough to make a paste.

In another jug put 1-2 GF stock cubes in 500ml of water (I find you sometimes need more stock cubes to flavour fully when you use the gluten-free variety. Also, you can use either filtered water or, to add extra vitamins, you can use the water from the pan that you steamed your other vegetables in).

Finally, over a high heat, add the skimmed meat juices and cornflour, whisk continuously and pour in stock water until the mixture thickens.

Optional

Depending on personal preferences, you may find you need to add in either more cornflour to thicken, more stock to flavour or a few drops of gravy browning to colour.

You can also add bone broth to your gravy if you have any in the freezer from stock previously made (see chicken broth recipe).

Yorkshire Puddings

Ingredients (makes 12)

- 4oz plain GF flour
- pinch salt
- 4 eggs
- DF milk (rice milk works well)

Directions (30 minutes)

Mix flour, salt, and eggs, and then add milk until mixture is the consistency of custard. Make at least one hour before needed and then add cold water until mixture is the consistency of thin custard! Heat oven to 200 degrees, put a small amount of oil into each muffin tin, and put in oven until the oil is really hot. Remove from the oven and pour mixture halfway up each tin then put straight back into oven for about 25 minutes. NEVER open oven door whilst they are cooking or they won't rise.

Honey Roast Root Vegetables

Par boil similar sized chunks of butternut squash, sweet potato, and swede. Heat some coconut oil on a baking tray in a very hot oven (around 220 degrees). Place the vegetables in the oil (the oil should be hot enough so they sizzle when you put them on the baking tray). Drizzle with honey and a little bit of thyme and roast in the oven for around 20-30 minutes. You can do carrots and parsnips in the same way (cut in sticks rather than cubes) but they will take less cooking and par boiling time.

Roast Potatoes

For fluffy roast potatoes, my friend Sarah gave me the following tip. After you have par boiled your potatoes and drained them, put the pan containing the potatoes (and no water) back on the stove top and shake the pan a bit. Steam will rise as the excess water evaporates from the potatoes and the edges will scuff a bit as you shake.

Pea and Mint Puree

Boil your peas and then puree half of them in a blender with olive oil, lemon zest and chopped fresh mint. Mix the puree with the whole peas and drizzle a little extra olive oil and squeeze of lemon. Garnish with fresh mint. Delicious!

Mediterranean Vegetables

My mum serves this a lot and you can do it with any vegetables really: try courgettes, peppers, tomatoes, onions and aubergine. Chopped, drizzled in olive oil and roasted in the oven.

Homemade Apple Pie

There is nothing like homemade apple pie after a roast dinner
(served with dairy-free ice cream of course!)

Ingredients (serves 6)

- 8 apples, peeled, cored, and sliced into small pieces
- 2 tsp cornflour
- 3 tbsp golden granulated sugar
- 1 tsp cinnamon
- 1 egg

Directions (40 minutes)

Line a flat round dish with pastry (see below), throw in the chopped
apples, 3 tbsp sugar and 1 tsp of cinnamon. Sprinkle two level tsp
cornflour to absorb juices. Roll the top of the pastry lid flat and place
on top. Wet the edges and pinch together so they stick. Cut two or
three vent holes in the lid. Whisk an egg with a dash of DF milk and
glaze the top of the pie. Bake in the oven at 200 degrees C for 30
minutes or until golden brown.

Optional

You can add other fruit such as blueberries, raspberries, rhubarb or
raisins to this recipe as well.

Gluten and Dairy-Free Pastry

Ingredients

- 200g GF plain flour
- 100g DF spread
- 4 tbsp water

Directions

The general principle with pastry is to make quantities in a ratio of double the flour to fat. Also bear in mind that gluten-free flour will absorb more water than conventional flour so add a few more drops of water if necessary.

Measure the ingredients into separate bowls, add the DF spread to the flour in chunks then mix the ingredients together (best to mix with your hands) until it becomes a consistency similar to breadcrumbs. At this point, add a few drops of water until it sticks together.

Roll the pastry out, dusting the rolling pin with GF flour to prevent it sticking.

CONCLUSION

Thank you for reading my book! This project has been my first foray into writing and I have found it cathartic and immensely enjoyable to get down on paper what I have learned over the years.

The most important thing I have learned is that nutrition (as with medicine) is not an exact science and 'expert' opinion can vary widely. There are some things we definitely know and some things we are still learning. Note that the contents of this book are not intended to replace medical advice specific to individual circumstances; you must always consult your doctor.

I have extensively researched and referenced this book in full to try and paint the most accurate and up to date picture, but would gratefully receive feedback regarding any errors (typos, clinical or otherwise). Please feel free to email me on gisellewrigley@outlook.com.

Wishing you nutritional health and happiness: I sincerely hope that reading this book has helped you to go gluten and dairy free and feel great!

REFERENCES

Introduction

1. http://www.allergyuk.org/common-food-intolerances/
   common-food-intolerances

2. 'Food intolerance could afflict half of UK.' *The Telegraph.* 15ᵗʰ Oct, 2009. http://www.telegraph.co.uk/
   foodanddrink/6336493/Food-intolerance-could-afflict-half-of-UK.html

3. Britt, Hannah. 'Novak Djokovic, going gluten free was a real game changer.' *The Express.* September 10ᵗʰ, 2013. http://
   www.express.co.uk/life-style/health/428272/Novak-Djokovic-Going-gluten-free-was-a-real-game-changer

PART ONE

Allergies

1. Farlex. 'Allergies.' *The Free Dictionary.* http://medical-dictionary.thefreedictionary.com/Allergies

2. 'Food Allergy.' *NHS Choices.* http://www.nhs.uk/conditions/
   food-allergy/Pages/Intro1.aspx

3. Ibid.

4. Bradley, Jeanette. 'The 8 most common food allergens.'

About Health. http://foodallergies.about.com/od/foodallergybasics/a/big_eight_fa.htm

5. Mosby. 'Atopy.' *Mosby's Medical Dictionary.*

6. H Okada, C Kuhn, H Feillet, J-F Bach. 'The hygiene hypothesis for autoimmune and allergic diseases: an update.' *Clinical and Experimental Immunology.* April 2010: 160 (1) 1-9 http://www.ncbi.nlm.nih.gov/pmc/articles/PMC2841828/

7. Ibid.

8. Mellowship, Dawn. 'About Leaky Gut.' *The Leaky Gut Syndrome.* http://www.leakygut.co.uk/About%20Leaky%20Gut.htm

9. 'Leaky Gut Syndrome.' *NHS Choices.* http://www.nhs.uk/Conditions/leaky-gut-syndrome/Pages/Introduction.aspx

10. Syed A., Kohli A., Nadean K.C., 'Food allergy and diagnosis therapy: where are we now?' *Immunotherapy.* Sept 2013; 5 (9):931-944 http://www.ncbi.nlm.nih.gov/pmc/articles/PMC4121393/

11. Gazzola, Alex, *Living with food intolerance and living with food allergy.* (Great Britain, Sheldon Press, 2008) http://www.ion.ac.uk/information/onarchives/diagnosingallergy

12. Ibid.

13. Farlex. 'Anaphylaxis.' *The Free Dictionary.* http://medical-dictionary.thefreedictionary.com/Anaphylaxis

14. Leiberman, Phil, MD. The severity of a future anaphylactic reaction to foods cannot be predicted by the severity of a previous reaction. *American Academy of Asthma, Allergy and Immunology. 15th Sept, 2012.* https://www.aaaai.org/ask-the-expert/severity-future-anaphylactic-reaction.aspx

15. Syed, Aleena, Kohli, Arunima, Nadean, Kari, C., Food allergy and diagnosis therapy: where are we now? *Immunotherapy.* Sept 2013; 5 (9):931-944 http://www.ncbi.nlm.nih.gov/pmc/articles/PMC4121393/

16. Ibid.

17. Dower, Moira. 'Allergies Health Centre.' *Web MD Health News.* http://www.webmd.boots.com/allergies/news/20100810/nice-allergy-guidance

18. Netting, Merryn, Makrides, Maria, Gold, Michael, Quinn, Patrick ad Penttila, Irmeli, 'Heated Allergens and Induction of Tolerance in Food Allergic Children.' *Nutrients.* June 2013: 5 (6):2028-2046. http://www.ncbi.nlm.nih.gov/pmc/articles/PMC3725491/

19. Staden U., Rolinck-Werminghaus C.,Brewe F., Wahn U., Niggemann B., Beyer K., 'Specific oral tolerance induction in food allergy in children: efficacy and clinical patterns of reaction.' Allergy. Nov 2007: 62 (11):1261-9. http://www.ncbi.nlm.nih.gov/pubmed/17919140/

20. Begin P., Dominiguez T., Wilson S.P., Bacal C., Mehrotra A., Kausch B., Trela A., Tavassoli M., Hoyte E., O'Riordan G., Blakemore A., Seki S., Hamilton R.G., Nadeau K.C.

'Phase 1 results of safety and tolerability in a rush oral immunotherapy protocol to multiple foods using Omalizumab. *Allergy, Asthma and Clinical Immunology*. Feb 2014; 10 (1): 7. http://www.ncbi.nlm.nih.gov/pubmed/24576338

21. Ofani I.M., Begin P., Kearney C., Dominguez T.L., Mehrotra A., Bacal L.R., Wilson S., Nadeau K., Multiple allergen oral immunotherapy improves quality of life in caregivers of food allergic pediatric subjects. *Journal of Allergy and Asthma Clinical Immunology*. May 2014; 10 (1): 25. http://www.ncbi.nlm.nih.gov/pubmed/24860608

22. Varshney P., Jones S.M., Scurlock A.M., Perry T.T., Kemper A., Steele P., Hiegel A., Kamilaris J., Carlisle S., Yue X., Kulis M., Pons L., Vickery B., Burks., A.W., 'A randomised controlled study on peanut oral immunotherapy: clinical desensitisation and modulation of the allergic response. *Journal of Allergy Clinical Immunology Practice*. Mar 2011; 127 (3): 654-60. http://www.ncbi.nlm.nih.gov/pubmed/21377034

23. Marcellin, L. Dr., 'Outgrowing Allergies.' *Everyday health*. http://www.everydayhealth.com/year-round-allergies/developing-or-outgrowing-allergies.aspx

24. Sampson, H. A., Peanut oral immunotherapy: is it ready for clinical practice? *Journal of Allergy Clinical Immunology Practice*. Jan 2013; 1 (1): 15-21. http://www.ncbi.nlm.nih.gov/pubmed/24229817

25. 'About Coeliac Disease.' *Coeliac UK*. https://www.coeliac.org.uk/coeliac-disease/about-coeliac-disease-and-dermatitis-herpetiformis/

Intolerances

1. 'What is food intolerance?' *Allergy UK.* http://www.allergyuk. org/food-intolerance/what-is-food-intolerance

2. Ibid.

3. Common food intolerances.' *Allergy UK.* http://www.aller-gyuk.org/common-food-intolerances/common-food-intolerances

4. 'Gluten free diet appeals to 30% of adults, survey says.' *The Huffington Post.* 2rd June, 2013. http://www.huffingtonpost. com/2013/03/06/gluten-free-diet_n_2818954.html5

5. 'Should you cut out bread to stop bloating?' *NHS Choices.* http://www.nhs.uk/Livewell/digestive-health/Pages/cutting-out-bread.aspx?app_data=%7B%22pi%22%3A%2257840_ 1411574642_251105096%22%2C%22pt%22%3A%22twit-ter%22%7D

6. Matthews S. B., Waud J.P., Roberts A.G., Campbelll A.K., 'Systemic lactose intolerance: a new perspective on an old problem.' Postgrad Medical Journal. 2005; 81: 167-173. http:// pmj.bmj.com/content/81/953/167.full.pdf

7. Ibid.

8. Ibid.

9. Mandal, A. Dr, 'Lactose intolerance history.' *News Medical.* http://www.news-medical.net/health/Lactose-Intolerance-History.aspx

10. Grand R.J., Montgomery R.K., 'Lactose malabsorption.' *Current Treatment Options Gastroenterology*. Feb 2008; 11 (1): 19-25. http://www.ncbi.nlm.nih.gov/pubmed/21063860

11. Skypala, I., Vlieg Boestra B., 'Food intolerance and allergy: increased incidence or contemporary inadequate diets?' *Current Opinion in Clinical Nutrition and Metabolic Care*. Sept 2014; 17 (5): 442-7. http://www.ncbi.nlm.nih.gov/pubmed/25003529

12. Barrett J.S., Gibson P.R., FODMAPS and non-allergenic food intolerance: FODMAPS or food chemicals?' *Therapeutic Advanced Gastroenterology*. Jul 2012; 5 (4):261-8. http://www.ncbi.nlm.nih.gov/pubmed/22778791

13. 'Identifying your food intolerances.' *Allergy UK*. http://www.allergyuk.org/food-intolerance/identifying-your-food-intolerances

14. Ibid.

15. 'About Coeliac Disease.' *Coeliac UK*. https://www.coeliac.org.uk/coeliac-disease/getting-diagnosed/

16. Matthews S. B., Waud J.P., Roberts A.G., Campbell A.K., 'Systemic lactose intolerance: a new perspective on an old problem.' *Postgrad Medical Journal*. 2005; 81: 167-173. http://pmj.bmj.com/content/81/953/167.full.pdf

17. Gazzola, Alex, *Living with food intolerance and living with food allergy*. (Great Britain, Sheldon Press, 2005) http://www.ion.ac.uk/information/onarchives/diagnosingallergy

18. Ibid.

19. Ibid.

20. Professor Jonathan Brostoff and Linda Gamlin, *The Complete Guide to Food Allergy and Intolerance,* (Great Britain: Bloomsbury Publishing, 1998), 114-115.

21. Millichap J.G., Yee M.M., 'The diet factor in pediatric and adolescent migraine.' *Pediatric Neurology*. Jan 2003; 28 (1); 9-15. http://www.ncbi.nlm.nih.gov/pubmed/12657413

22. Erin Baloudis, "The FODMAP Diet", *JHP Magazine*, October 2013, 74-80

23. El- Salhy M., Gilja O.H., Gunderson D., Hatlebakk J.G., Haushen T., 'Interaction between ingested nutrients and gut endocrine cells in patients with irritable bowel syndrome (a review).' *Journal of Molecular Medicine.* Aug 2014 ; 34 (2): 363-71. http://www.ncbi.nlm.nih.gov/pubmed/24939595

24. Jockers, Dr David, 'Are you experiencing a healing crisis?' *Natural News.* August 28th, 2012. http://www.naturalnews.com/036968_healing_crisis_detoxification_liver_health.html

25. 'What is food intolerance.' *Allergy UK.* http://www.allergyuk.org/food-intolerance/what-is-food-intolerance

PART TWO

Healthy made EASY

1. Gunnars, Kris, '9 ways that processed foods are killing people.' *Authority Nutrition.* http://authoritynutrition.com/9-ways-that-processed-foods-are-killing-people/

2. Smith-Spangler C., Brandean M.L., Hunter G.E., Bavinger J.C., Pearson M., Eschbach P.J., Sandaram V., Liu H., Schimer P., Stave C., Olkin I., Bravata D.M., 'Are organic foods safer or healthier than conventional alternatives? A systematic review.' Annals of Internal Medicine. Sept 2012; 157 (5): 348-66. http://www.ncbi.nlm.nih.gov/pubmed/22944875

3. Duckett SK, Neel JP, Fontenot JP, Clapham WM, 'Effects of winter stocker growth rate and finishing system on: III. Tissue proximate, fatty acid, vitamin and cholesterol content.' *Journal of Animal Science.* May 2009; 87 (9): 2961–70. http://www.journalofanimalscience.org/content/87/9/2961

4. Wall R., Ross R.P., Fitzgerald G.F., Stanton C., 'Fatty acids from fish: the anti-inflammatory potential of long-chain omega 3 fatty acids.' *Nutrition Reviews.* May 2010; 68 (5): 280-9. http://www.ncbi.nlm.nih.gov/pubmed/20500789

5. Tsuji M., 'Useful biomarkers for assessing the adverse health effects of PCBs in allergic children: pediatric molecular epidemiology.' *Environmental Health Preventative Medicine.* Oct 2014. http://www.ncbi.nlm.nih.gov/pubmed/25344634

6. 'Dirty Dozen and Clean 15'. *Environmental Working Group.* http://www.ewg.org/foodnews/

7. Simopoulos A.P.,'The importantce of the ratio of omega 6 to omega 3 essential fatty acids.' *Biomedical Pharmacotherapeutics.* Oct 2002; 56 (8):365-79. http://www.ncbi.nlm.nih.gov/pubmed/12442909

8. Mosley M. Dr, 'Michael Mosley: Should people be eating more fat?' *BBC News Magazine.* 15th October, 2014. http://www.bbc.co.uk/news/magazine-29616418

9. 'The definitive guide to cooking with fat.' *Caveman Doctor.* May 27th, 2012. http://ww.cavemandoctor.com/2012/05/27/checking-your-oil-the-definitive-guide-to-cooking-with-fat/

10. 'Healthy Eating Plate and Healthy Eating Pyramid.' Harvard School of Public Health. http://www.hsph.harvard.edu/nutritionsource/healthy-eating-plate/

11. Hogervorst J.G., Schouten L.J., Lenings E.J., Goldbohm R.A., Van den Brandt P.A., 'A prospective study of dietary acrylamide intake and the risk of endometrial, ovarian and breast cancer.' *Cancer Epidemiology Biomarker Prevention.* Nov 2007; 16 (11): 2304-13. http://www.ncbi.nlm.nih.gov/pubmed/18006919

12. Helen Foster, *GI Basics,* (Great Britain: Octopus Publishing Group, 2006), p 10-11.

13. Atkins, R.C. Dr, *Dr Atkins New Diet Revolution*, (Great Britain: Vermilion, 2003).

14. Mosley, M. Dr, *The Fast Diet: The Secret of Intermittent Fasting – Lose Weight, Stay Healthy, Live Longer.* (Great Britain: Short Books, 2013)

15. Knapton, Sarah. 'Eat within a 12 hour window to lose weight say scientists.' *The Telegraph.* 2nd December 2014. http://www.telegraph.co.uk/health/dietandfitness/11268685/Eat-within-12-hour-window-to-lose-weight-say-scientists.html

16. Cordain, Loren, *The Paleo Diet.* (Great Britain: Houghton Mifflin Harcourt, 2010).

17. 'A Healthy, Varied Diet.' British Nutrition Foundation. http://www.nutrition.org.uk/healthyliving/healthyeating/healthyvarieddiet

18. 'Healthy Eating Plate and Healthy Eating Pyramid.' Harvard School of Public Health. http://www.hsph.harvard.edu/nutritionsource/healthy-eating-plate/

19. Mosley, 'Michael Mosley: Should people be eating more fat?'

20. Messina M., Redmond G., 'Effects of soy protein and soybean isoflavones on thyroid function in healthy adults and hypothyroid patients: a review of the relevant literature.' *Thyroid.* Mar 2006; 16 (3): 249-58. http://www.ncbi.nlm.nih.gov/pubmed/16571087

21. Gunnars, Kris, 'Is soy bad or good for you? The shocking truth.' *Authority Nutrition.* http://authoritynutrition.com/is-soy-bad-for-you-or-good/

22. Winslow, Amelia. 'Lactose intolerant? What can you eat?'

Eating Made Easy. March 26, 2011 http://eating-made-easy. com/2011/03/26/lactose-intolerant-what-can-you-eat/

Supplements

Omega 3

1. Delgado-Lista J, Perez-Martinez P, Lopez-Miranda J, Perez-Jimenez F (June 2012). "Long chain omega-3 fatty acids and cardiovascular disease: a systematic review". *The British Journal of Nutrition*. 107 Suppl 2: S201–13. http://journals. cambridge.org/action/displayAbstract?fromPage=online&aid=8586737&fileId=S0007114512001596

2. Calder, P.C., 'n-3 Polyunsaturated fatty acids, inflammation and inflammatory diseases.' Americal Journal of Clinical Nutrition. June 2006; 83 (6): 51505-15195. http://ajcn. nutrition.org/content/83/6/S1505.short

3. Duckett SK, Neel JP, Fontenot JP, Clapham WM, 'Effects of winter stocker growth rate and finishing system on: III. Tissue proximate, fatty acid, vitamin and cholesterol content.' *Journal of Animal Science*. May 2009; 87 (9): 2961–70. http:// www.journalofanimalscience.org/content/87/9/2961

4. Davidson P., Meyers G.J., Weiss B., 'Mercury Exposure and Child Development Outcomes.' *Pediatrics*. April 2014; 113 (4); 1-23-1029.

5. Sachs, F. Dr, 'Ask the Expert: Omega 3 Fatty Acids.' *Harvard School of Public Health*. http://www.hsph.harvard.edu/ nutritionsource/omega-3/

6. Calder, P.C., 'n-3 Polyunsaturated fatty acids, inflammation and inflammatory diseases.' Americal Journal of Clinical Nutrition. June 2006; 83 (6): 51505-15195. http://ajcn.nutrition.org/content/83/6/S1505.short

7. Northup, C. Dr, 'Now saturated fat is good for you?' *Huffington Post.* 26th March, 2014. http://www.huffingtonpost.com/christiane-northrup/saturated-fat_b_4914235.html

8. 'Saturated Fat Heart Disease 'Myth'' *BBC News Health.* http://www.bbc.co.uk/news/health-24625808

9. Yeap S.K., Beh B.K., Ali N.M., Yusof H.M., Ho W.Y., Koh S.P., Alitheen N.B., Lang K., 'Antistress and antioxidant effects of virgin coconut oil in vivo.' *Experimental and Therapeutic Medicine.* Jan 2015; 9 (1):39-42. http://www.ncbi.nlm.nih.gov/pubmed/25452773

10. Mosley M. Dr., 'Michael Mosley: Should people be eating more fat?' *BBC News Magazine.* 15th October, 2014. http://www.bbc.co.uk/news/magazine-29616418

Probiotics

1. Professor Jonathan Brostoff and Linda Gamlin, *The Complete Guide to Food Allergy and Intolerance,* (Great Britain: Bloomsbury Publishing, 1998), p 245.

2. Dietrich C. G., Kottmann T., Alvai M., 'Commercially available probiotic drinks containing lactobacillus casei reduce antibiotic associated diarrhoea.' *World Journal of*

Gastroenterology. Nov 2014; 20 (42): 15837-44. http://www. ncbi.nlm.nih.gov/pubmed/25400470

3. Guandalini S., Cemat E., Moscosco D., ' Prebiotics and probiotics in IBS and inflammatory bowel disease in children.' *Beneficial Microbes.* Nov 2014; 12:1-9. https://www.ncbi.nlm. nih.gov/pubmed/25391345

4. Ford A.C., Quigley E.M., Lacy B.E., Lembo A.J., Saito Y.A., Soffer E.E. Spiege B.M. Moayyeti P., Schiller L.R., 'Efficacy of prebiotics and probiotics and synbiotics in irritable bowel syndrome and chronic idiopathic constipation: systematic review and meta analysis. *American Journal of Gastroenterology.* Oct 2014; 109 (10): 1547-61. https://www. ncbi.nlm.nih.gov/pubmed/25070051

Calcium and Vitamin D

1. Keet C.A., Malsui E.C., Savage J.H., Neurman-Sunshine D., Skripak J., Peng R.D., Wood, R., 'Potential mechanism for the association between fall birth and food allergy.' *Allergy.* June 2012; 67 (6):775-782. http://www.ncbi.nlm.nih.gov/pmc/ articles/PMC3349789/

2. Joanna Caines, Debbie Evans and Mary Feeney, (Sept 2009). 'Calcium: Are you Getting Enough?' *Food Allergy and Intolerance Specialist Group: Part of The British Dietetic Association.* (5th Floor, Charles House, 148/0 Great Charles Street, Queensway, Birmingham, B33HT)

3. Pines A., Langer R.D., 'The cardiovascular safety aspects of calcium supplementation; where dose the truth lie?'

Climacteric. Oct 2014; 16:1-5. https://www.ncbi.nlm.nih.gov/pubmed/25318377

4. Kuanrang L., Rudolf K., Jakob L, Sabine R., 'Association of dietary calcium intake and calcium supplementation with myocardial infarction and stroke risk. Heart. Feb 2012; 98:920-925. http://heart.bmj.com/content/98/12/920.short?g=w_heart_current_tab

Digestive Enzymes

1. Di Stefano M, Miceli E, Gotti S, Missanelli A, Mazzoccahi S, Corazza GR (January 2007). "The effect of oral alpha-galactosidase on intestinal gas production and gas-related symptoms". *Dig. Dis. Sci.* **52** (1): 78–83. Di Stefano M, Miceli E, Gotti S, Missanelli A, Mazzoccahi S, Corazza GR (January 2007). "The effect of oral alpha-galactosidase on intestinal gas production and gas-related symptoms". *Dig. Dis. Sci.* **52** (1): 78–83. Di Stefano M, Miceli E, Gotti S, Missanelli A, Mazzoccahi S, Corazza GR (January 2007). "The effect of oral alpha-galactosidase on intestinal gas production and gas-related symptoms". *Dig. Dis. Sci.* **52** (1): 78–83. Di Stefano M, Miceli E, Gotti S, Missanelli A, Mazzoccahi S, Corazza GR (January 2007). "The effect of oral alpha-galactosidase on intestinal gas production and gas-related symptoms". *Dig. Dis. Sci.* **52** (1): 78–83.Di Stefano M., Miceli E., Gotti S., Missanelli A., Mazzocchi S., Corazza G.R., ' The effect of oral alpha galactosidase on intestinal gas production and gas related symptoms.' *Digestive Disease Sciences.* Jan 2007; 52 (11): 78-83. http://link.springer.com/article/10.1007%2Fs10620-006-9296-9

2. Ganiats T.G., Norcross W.A., Halverson A.L., Burford P.A., Palinkas L.A., 'Does Beano prevent gas? A double blind crossover study of oral alpha galactosidase to treat dietary oligosaccharide intolerance.' *Journal of Family Practice.* Nov 1994; 39 (5):441-4. http://www.ncbi.nlm.nih.gov/m/pubmed/7964541/

Antioxidants

1. Chatzi L., Apostolaki G., Bibakis I, Skypala I., Babaki –Laikai V., Tzanalus N., Kogeunas M., Cullinan P., 'Protective effect of fruits and vegetables and the mediterranean diet on asthma and allergies among children in Crete.' *Thorax.* Aug 2007; (218): 677-83. http://www.ncbi.nlm.nih.gov/m/pubmed/17412780/?i=3&from=/20522849/related

2. Rosenlund H., Magnusson J., Kull I., Hakannson N., Wolk A., Pershagen G., Wickman M., Bergstrom A., 'Antioxidant intake and allergic disease in children.' *Clinical and Experimental Alllergy.* Oct 2012; 42 (10):1491-500. http://www.ncbi.nlm.nih.gov/m/pubmed/22994346/?i=4&from=/25097022/related

3. 'Superfoods for Optimal Health.' *Web MD.* http://www.webmd.com/food-recipes/antioxidants-your-immune-system-super-foods-optimal-health

Food as Medicine

1. Tattleman. E., 'Health effects of garlic.' American Family Physician. Jul 2005; 72 (1):103-6. http://www.ncbi.nlm.nih.gov/m/pubmed/16035690/?i=6&from=/20120123/related

2. Rennard B., Gossman G., Robbins R., Rennard S. 'Chicken Soup Inhibits Neutrophil Chemotaxis In Vitro.' *Chest*. 2000; 118: 1150-1157. http://www.unmc.edu/publicrelations/chickensoup_newsrelease.htm

3. Hyman M., Dr, Blum S, Bender M., *The Immune System Recovery Plan: A Doctor's 4 Step Program to Treat Autoimmune Disease.* (Great Britain: Scribner Book Company: Apr 2013).

4. Underwood A., 'The new superfoods.' *Newsweek.* 24th Oct 2005; 146 (17):79-80.

PART THREE

Recipes

1. Garcia-Estepa RM, Guerra-Hernandex E, Garcia-Villanova B. Phytic acid content in milled cereal products and breads. *Food Research International*. 1999; 32(3):217-21.

2. 'High cholesterol.' British Heart Foundation. http://www.bhf.org.uk/heart-health/conditions/high-cholesterol.aspx

3. Gunnars, Kris. '6 reasons why eggs are the healthiest food on the planet.' *Authority Nutrition.* http://authoritynutrition.com/6-reasons-why-eggs-are-the-healthiest-food-on-the-planet/

4. Daniel, Kaalya, PhD, 'Why Broth is Beautiful: Essential Roles for Proline, Glycine and Gelatin.' *The Weston A Price*

Foundation, June 18th, 2003. http://www.westonaprice.org/health-topics/why-broth-is-beautiful-essential-roles-for-proline-glycine-and-gelatin/

5. Lydia, 'Bone Broth, Nutritional Facts and Benefits.' *Divine Health from the Inside Out*. May 23rd, 2012 http://divinehealthfromtheinsideout.com/2012/05/bone-broth-nutritional-facts-benefits/

NOTES:

....

....

....

....

....

....

....

....

....

....

....

....

....

Made in the USA
Monee, IL
26 September 2019